SURVIVING

SPIKE MILLIGAN

SURVIVING
SPIKE MILLIGAN

**Writing with Spike –
the agony, the ecstasy . . .
the jam doughnuts!**

JOHN ANTROBUS

ROBSON BOOKS

791.092   2026889

This paperback edition first published in Great Britain in 2003 by Robson Books, The Chrysalis Building, Bramley Road, London W10 6SP

An imprint of **Chrysalis** Books Group plc

British Library Cataloguing in Publication Data
A catalogue record for this title is available from the British Library.

ISBN 1 86105 676 1

Typeset by SX Composing DTP, Rayleigh, Essex
Printed by Bell & Bain Ltd, Glasgow

to Nicole . . .

ACKNOWLEDGEMENTS

With thanks to all these people . . .

Jane Donovan, Senior Editor, Robson Books, and to all the helpful Robson team, may I say Premier League material.

To the Writers' Guild of Great Britain for help on contractual matters. If you are a writer, join today.

To the Royal Literary Fund for financial assistance.

To Marijka Goode at the Beeb for ferreting out scripts and tapes.

To my beloved Nicole Souchal who, as always, typed up my long-hand tea-stained pages… and to Robert at Valeries, Soho, who provided the tea stains and hopefully (at the time of writing) the venue for the book launch.

To Dr Howard Gotlieb, Mugar Memorial Library, Boston University, USA, who collects my original manuscripts and provides research material as required.

To John Calder for permission to use an extract of 'An Apple A Day' from *Why Bournemouth?* & *Other Plays*, Calder & Boyars Ltd (1970).

To any I have overlooked, my apologies.

And naturally to Jeremy Robson, the indefatigable publisher and my friend, who had the perspicacity to see the amazing potential in this book.

And finally to you, dear reader, without whom this enterprise is lost.

PART I

TICK, TOCK, WHAT?

'All things be ready if the mind be so.'

Shakespeare

'It's all in the mind, folks!'

Milligan

'Tick, tock, what?'

Antrobus

There was Spike.
There was me.
Then there was me and Spike.
There was history.
There was war.
There was Spike as a soldier.
There was me as a schoolboy.
Then there was me and Spike, writing together.

There was memory then and memory now. Then the past remembered was different. Spike, a shell-shocked soldier...

Spike: I was standing on a beach. This plane swooped low over our camp, out to sea. I said crash you bastard. Crash! And the plane crashed into the water.

Me: I was looking out of the window. I thought there must be more to life than this. Killing people. That's what I'm being trained for. Bayonet practice. Sacks of straw. It's not real. But when it becomes real it will be too late to say no. So I left Sandhurst and they let me go. They thought I was mad or religious. But not wanting to kill people was a disadvantage.

Spike and me writing together.

Spike: He was a dwarf. She left me for a dwarf.
Me: Was he in a circus ?
Spike: No.

Me: In class I was looking out of the window. Such a nice day. I thought there's got to be more to life than this...

Spike: Early one morning. Running on the track at Alexandra Palace. I felt marvellous. It was a moment when I felt wonderful. There was no-one else out there. The best moment in my life. Just running on that track in the early morning...

Spike and I writing. No phone calls. It's off the hook. The door's locked. It's our world for as long as Spike can keep the rest out of his head...

Where are we? Memory without location. First thoughts.

She said, 'Don't go up. Spike's not seeing anyone. He's locked his door.'
        I went up anyway and knocked.
        'Spike.'
        He opened the door. 'Come in,' he said. 'The bastards have got me.' His hair was tousled. 'I slept here last night. I didn't go home.'
        'If you don't want to work...'
        'No. We'll work.'
        In half an hour we were laughing as we wrote whatever that was.

Letter to *The Times*. Letter to the *Manchester Guardian*. Spike was always writing letters to the papers. He wanted to save buildings. When they were being demolished he went along with Bill Kerr (the famous Australian comedian, 'I'm only here for four minutes' the Windmill) – or on his own – and rescued things, fireplaces, doorknobs, banisters, tiles. He stole them if necessary or gave five bob to some bloke who said help yourself, Spike. Bill Kerr had a big laugh. He was always being chased out of bedrooms or hiding in wardrobes but he survived the husbands.

'He won't see anyone today.'

I went up anyway.

'Spike.'

He let me in. 'Come in, John. Keep the other bastards out. They'll kill me.'

He took down a box file. He had shelves full of box files in his office. She won't stop spending, he said. She's ruining me. Harrods. He was on the phone. Something about a lawn mower. It had to be repaired. He whispered hoarsely into the phone, 'Well, come and collect it. Yes, I will abandon my work, my career, my life and I will be there to let you in so that you can take it away.' He put the phone down. 'That man gets paid from nine to five six days a week to think about lawn mowers all bloody day and he still has time to destroy me. Him and all the others.'

'If you don't want to write today…'

'Yes.'

In half an hour we were laughing.

'Go and get some jam doughnuts, will you? Here's some money,' said Spike.

'How many?'

'Six. Three each.'

Spike always had money. Cash lying around. In his Mini he had cash scattered around on the floor of the car…

In his Mini. Spike is tailgate-ing some 'bastard' who has cut him in.

'How do you like a taste of your own medicine?' he snarls.

He accelerates when the car in front accelerates, slowing when it slows, glued to within a few feet or inches of the offending 'bastard' motorist.

Me: Spike… (*nervous laugh*) Could you go slower?

Spike slows to about thirteen miles an hour. The car in front escapes.

'How's that?'

'Alright.'

He slows further to a dangerous eight miles an hour, nursing the car along in little spasms.

'Better?'

Shelagh says, 'Spike, stop it. You're making John nervous.'

We arrive somewhere. Spike leaps out of the car with an energy that produces light in the dark parking space.

'I've never had an accident,' he says. 'I'm aware of everything that's happening on the road and nobody gets away with it.'

Purged, we enter the restaurant and have a hilarious evening.

That surfacing fragment of time is out of sequence. Shelagh is much later. Wife number three (obviously on my side). And Minis aren't yet off the production line.

Back to Shepherd's Bush. Fog. I can't see my hand in front of me. It's before the Clean Air Act. Motoring was different in the fifties…

I'm downstairs waiting for Spike – where is he? – and in walks Ray Galton, in the height of fashion.

Ray: Last night, what a pea-souper! Were you out in it?

Me: I don't know. It was too foggy to tell.

Ray: I was with Alan. He had to walk in front of the car. We were on our way to Morden. It was so bad we had to stay at my sister's house in Clapham Common.

Me: What was that like?

Ray: Oh, we get on alright.

Spike comes in. We go up to his office and sit around warming up the brain cells.

Me: Were you out in the fog last night, Spike?

Spike: Yes, it was terrible. My wife was coughing. I said you go on ahead and I'll follow. There's no point in us both getting run over. I said I'll be able to hear you, don't worry. When we got home I realised I'd been following the wrong cough.

Me: Was it another lady?

Spike: No, it was an Old Age Pensioner. We were somewhere near Highgate. He invited me in to stroke the cat.

Me: Did your wife get home alright?

Spike: I expect so. I haven't been back to look.

We don't seem to be in the mood for writing.

Me: Do you think you willed that plane to crash, Spike?

    Spike: Yes.

    Me: Are you claiming supernatural powers?

    Spike: No, I'm telling you what happened.

Spike: The clock stopped at 8.33 one evening. It was only hours later I discovered it was the exact time my mother died in Australia.

    Me: Did you have the clock repaired?

    Spike: No, I had my mother buried.

    Me: You could have had the clock buried and your mother repaired.

    Spike (*laughing*): It would have cost too much. She was only guaranteed against subsidence and flooding. Go and get some jam doughnuts.

    Me: How many?

    Spike: Six. Three each.

    There's a knock on the door.

    Spike: There's no-one here! We're dead!

    Voice off: It's an undertaker!

    Spike: Thank God.

    Spike opens the door and lets in Eric Sykes. They fall about laughing.

It's another day. When I emerge from the tube at Shepherd's Bush the fog has vanished and with it the ideal setting for sex murders. I'm wearing my *Rebel Without A Cause* James Dean leather jacket and I have a smile for the world. Perhaps it should have been a scowl but I can't get everything right all at once.

    I walk past Silver's, the tailors and gents' outfitters that are doing better business since Associated London Scripts started up a few doors down The Green and writers with money were looking to dress the part. Silver's was Show Biz, Danny Kaye at the Palladium, Johnny Ray and the doyen, Frank Sinatra. Step inside lads, we'll measure you up for fame and fortune. Johnny Speight was often in there, and Eric Sykes, the camelhair coat brigade. Spike might have bought a pair of socks there. I was marching to the beat of a different drum. So I waved and walked past their emporium with the ever open doors.

I squeeze past the vegetables and go up to the office, into reception.

I hear laughter and raspberries being blown.

'He's got Peter Sellers up there,' says Pam Vertue, our typist who has a lovely smile. She's the sister of Beryl Vertue, our agent.

'Spike,' I call up the stairs.

'Come up, John!'

I go up the narrow stairs with the balding green carpet and push open the door of Spike's office. Peter Sellers beams at me.

Peter: Hello, young John. Where have you come from?

Spike: He's come from downstairs.

Peter: But before then?

Me: I was born in Woolwich.

Peter: What took you so long to get here?

Spike: A tree fell on him. And he went to Sandhurst. John Antrobus was an officer cadet.

Peter: Really? What did they teach him?

Spice: They taught him to leave the army.

Peter: Just in time. Let's have lunch.

Later. At Bertorelli's.

Peter: I'm hoping to do a film with the Boulting Brothers. Are you available, Spike?

Spike: What for?

Peter: To be doing something else.

Spike: Definitely. I can be doing something else in Lewisham. Let me know the days you don't need me and I'll make sure I'm run over by a tram.

Peter: How about five days in June?

Spike: I'm already married to her.

Shouts to restaurant manager. Can you send us a fresh waiter please! This one's stained his trousers!

The waiter: These trousers came back from the cleaners this morning, Mr Milligan.

Spike: And you were still inside them, obviously.

Peter: He has to sleep somewhere, poor fellow.

Spike: What year is this wine?

Waiter: It's a Beaujolais 49, Spike.

Peter: Gad! It's getting late. I must phone my mother and tell her who I am. She doesn't like to entertain strangers.

Spike: Then you must send her a signed photograph of the Pope and tell her you've taken holy orders from the knees down.

Peter: What a splendid idea (*he blows a raspberry. As Major Bloodnok*). Nurse! The screens! Quickly!

Spike: Open a window, someone!

One day I met Harry Secombe in Spike's office.

'This is John Antrobus,' said Spike.

'Hello, Neddy!' shouted Harry as though encouraging Wales to score a try at Twickenham.

'He's from Sandhurst,' explained Spike.

'His knees must be blancoed!' exclaimed Harry.

'They are made of string.'

'The poor knotted fool!' Harry pulled a penny from his pocket, licked it and stuck it on his forehead, bursting into song, 'We'll keep a welcome in the hillside...' He sang all over my best suit.

Harry: Nice to meet you, laddy. Keep taking the tablets. Well, Spike, My Old Mukka, I must be going.

Spike: But you haven't arrived yet.

Harry: Good heavens! You mean... it's all a mirage? HeLLLLLPPP! The heat! The flies! The native women! Take this message on a stick to the BBC. I will be late for rehearsal tomorrow. Delayed in Africa. Love, Harry.

Spike (*as Eccles*): Right!

He tears up the piece of paper and stuffs it in his mouth.

Harry: What are you doing?

Spike: I'm eating the letter.

Harry: Why?

Spike: I can't read and I need the nourishment.

Harry: A wise precaution.

Spike: I always take precautions.

Harry: And you a good Catholic? Shame on you, Spike. Well, I must be going... No, I've done that bit (*he turns to me*). What did you say your name was?

Me: John.

Harry: Gad! In this light you looked like someone I know.

Spike: That's John Antrobus. I just introduced you to him.

Harry embraced me. 'You haven't changed a bit,' he said. 'Remarkable. For a moment I thought you were Florence Nightingale and I was going to ask for an enema. Farewell!'

And he fell down the stairs blowing raspberries, giggling and singing 'Wales! Wales! Glorious Wales…'

'I don't know who he is,' muttered Spike. 'But he's always on time.'

Johnny Speight had written his first joke for Edmundo Ros, 'Snow, snow, quick quick snow' and sensing that he could make a fortune moved into writing full-time. He had joined Associated London Scripts (ALS) a week before I had turned up fresh minted from the Royal Military Academy, Sandhurst.

ALS had been recently formed as a script-writing agency by Spike and Eric Sykes, plus Galton and Simpson. Frankie Howerd was also a director and he had brought along a business manager, whom it was rumoured had lost a testicle in the RAF during the war. Had he dropped it on Dresden?

The premises of ALS were over a greengrocers shop on Shepherd's Bush Green where old money changed hands and not too much of it. The local council were experimenting with litter on the windswept green but nobody thought it would catch on. Eric Sykes ate three eggs and chips daily in the local caff and Ray Galton and Alan Simpson were very tall and bent over slightly to talk to the rest of us. This was so that we would not feel intimidated and become aggressive. Alan was frightened of dying and short Scotsmen and knew that falling over was a long way to the ground. Ray was suave, always well dressed in a superior, Edwardian, *Clockwork Orange* fashion. He had an eye for the ladies whereas Alan guessed his mother was one. Alan, tall, dark and handsome, was no Flash Harry. You could never tell how he was playing his cards.

Into all this I was flung by a desire to be young, rich and famous. I was thrown in with men back from the war. Galton and Simpson had come from a tubercular sanatorium – thanks to streptomycin, the new wonder-drug. Beryl Vertue, who had been Ray and Alan's secretary, became our agent. She too had been in a tubercular sanatorium. We were all war-scarred. Well, even I had been bombed out at Exeter, 1943.

The BBC Radio Light Entertainement at Aeolian Hall, Bond Street, was a convalescent home for bomb happy ex-officers. One famous producer, well known for the urine stains on his trousers, had once stood above the trenches waving a stick encouraging his men, saying, 'There's nothing to be afraid of chaps!' when his head had been blown off. He didn't need it at the Beeb and found a decent salary, an office, a secretary and use of the lift. 'Run that past me again,' was his favourite line, as he mused, stuffing his tie into the bowl of his pipe and setting it alight.

'He's not seeing anyone today. His door's locked. I think he spent the night there.'

I went up anyway. On Spike's door was stuck a sign 'GO AWAY'. I knocked.

Me: It's me, Spike. Shall I go away?

Spike: Hang on, John.

Spike unlocked the door, let me in, then locked it again. 'I'm not very well,' he said. The curtains were drawn across and the desk lamp cast a pool of light on some cushions on the floor and a travelling blanket. The heat was on.

Me: Is it alright?

Spike: What?

Me: Me being here?

'Everybody's got to be somewhere,' he said. 'Did we arrange to meet?'

'Yes.'

Spike was slumped behind the desk, his hair wild, a stubble on his face.

Spike: What time is it?

Me: The third of November.

Spike: You could go and get some jam doughnuts.

Me: How many?

Spike: Six. They give energy to the brain. Nobody knows how much energy we burn up writing. I'm not well. If my leg was broken they'd see it and understand. But they can't see my mind. Tell them to make some tea, will you?

Me: OK.

I saw that the phone had been pulled out of the socket so all messages had to be relayed downstairs, or shouted down. I pointed at the phone… 'How did that happen, Spike?'

Spike: She wouldn't stop phoning me.

Me: You could have unplugged the phone on the switch-board downstairs.

Spike: Pulling it off the socket was quicker.

I laughed.

When I came back with the doughnuts and collected the tea on the way up, Pam asked me, 'Is it safe to breathe?'

'Oh, yes.'

I brought the refreshments into Spike's office and saw that he had pulled back the curtains. He blinked in the sunlight. 'Too much light. Too much noise,' he said.

We ate our doughnuts in silence and swigged the tea.

Head round the door, 'Hello Spike. Do you want the newspapers…'

'NO I DON'T!'

Spike slammed the door and locked it.

'You forgot to lock the door,' he said, accusingly.

'Sorry.'

'They'll get in. Any way they can. They've nothing better to do. Than to persecute genius. And I pay them to do it. A weekly salary to destroy me. Ten per cent of my earnings to bury me in trivial details. Just in case I don't get enough of it at home.'

He stared at the last doughnut.

'How many doughnuts have I had?'

'Three.'

'How many have you had?'

'Two.'

'Don't you want that last one?'

'No,' I said. 'You have it.'

'No,' he said. But Spike absent-mindedly licked the sugar off the last doughnut as I read out a story I had written the day before…

'Tick, Tock, What?'

'Tick, tock, what? Tick, tock, what?' said the old clock in the baronial hall.

'What?' demanded Sir Roger Grappling-Irons.

'Tick, tock, what? Tick, tock, what...'

'What?'

'Tick, tock, what...'

'What? What, what?' Sir Roger Grappling-Irons never got an answer from his clock. Tempted to destroy it though he was, he never did. Which was surprising because Sir Roger was always looking for ways to kill time. In fact he was famous and renowned as a Big Clock Hunter in Africa. There were many stuffed clocks in his hall, witness to the noble aristocrat's hobby.

It all started when he was a boy at Eton and someone suggested they had an hour to kill. He had immediately taken a shotgun and blown off the hour hand of the school clock. Later, rumour had it that he had killed Easter Bank Holiday Monday, 1923 outright and hidden it under his floorboards. Questions In Parliament. A cover up of course. There was no getting to the bottom of that story, except that it ends this one.

'Tick, tock, what...'

'What?'

'Tick, tock, what...'

'What? What? WHAT? In heaven's name will no-one rid me of this turbulent clock?'

'Brilliant,' said Spike. 'Nobody else will understand it. You'll see. You're the only other genius round here. Don't let them destroy you like they've destroyed me. Learn to be mundane, ordinary, boring, GREY. Then they'll leave you alone.' He reached for a box file.

'I'm not much in the mood for writing today,' he said. 'I need to phone Harrods to see how much she spent last month. It's a joint account.'

'You could close the account, Spike.'

'No. She'd find another way to get at me. This way at least I know what's going on. She knows she can spend what she likes. I'm trapped. I'm too ill to write. We'll all go down together, you'll see. Then she'll be happy. When I'm working for the Gas Board reading meters instead of Sean O'Casey, she'll be happy.'

Spike ordered a taxi and went home. He probably made it up with his then wife, June. They were not at loggerheads all the time. She was beautiful – a nice woman – and Spike had a big heart, but with the pressures he put himself under writing for the Goons something had to give… his domestic life could not soak up the stresses of his working life indefinitely.

I sat in his office awhile but I couldn't think of anything to write. So I went across the landing and talked to Ray Galton and Alan Simpson, then we went to lunch at Bertorelli's. Johnny Speight joined us and persuaded me that the only way he could pay me back the £15 he owed me was to borrow another fiver.

Ray said, 'Spike will be alright. He's been worse than that.'

'Yes,' said Alan. 'If he gets really bad he goes to the nursing home in Finchley.'

Spike went to the nursing home in Finchley and slept for some days but he eventually came back to the office complaining that the uncomprehending bastards had put him in a room next to the dustbins outside and the banging lids when they knew he needed SILENCE.

Larry Stephens was writing Goon shows with Spike when I arrived at the agency. I was employed in a team of writers on the Frankie Howerd Radio Show. Larry was an ex-marine who'd had a tough war and was drinking a lot of whisky. This would kill him soon but meanwhile he was a gentle amiable man. Spike told me…

'Larry and I made a tape while we were writing Goon shows. A tape of our farts. When we felt one coming on, we would turn the machine on and record it. I put some introductory music to this fart tape and one night at home when we had company for dinner I put it on. The music was pleasant background to the dinner conversation and June was well pleased with the way the evening was going. Then the farting began. I said nothing. The people packed up and went home. Good riddance.

Boring bunch of my wife's friends. They had no conversation anyway.'

Spike was back sleeping in his office for a few days as a result of his wife and himself taking a different view of the evening. But Spike was in high spirits. He had beaten mediocrity and it made a great story.

Me and Spike. I was younger than, a mere youth of 21 breaking in upon the scriptwriting scene, the boy wonder. I did not know that I was already using alcohol not as most used it, socially, but to transform my emotional landscape from shy boy to in your face fuck off I'm your working class socialist, don't you know, newly invented Sarf London accent and ditched Sandhurst modulations and Tory opinions. I was a friend of Johnny Speight, admirer of Stalin. I read Henri Bergson's *Theory Of Creative Evolution*, Bernard Shaw and Trotsky and pissed it up against the wall with my new-found money and left wing opinions. And Johnny was a good friend to have but some said he was my Svengali. Put bluntly I was impressionable, looking to build a whole new character for myself, one that even I could believe in. God is dead and satire is King and bollocks to the Establishment. Let's say I got carried away and had no idea of my true agenda which was to fix myself with all the trappings of success. I got on to Albert Camus, *The Outsider*. That's what I was, an existentialist! I loved Jean Paul Sartre's *Iron In The Soul*. All good stuff…

A way to go to alcoholic breakdown, unemployment, degredation and isolation from myself, from my fellow man and from God. But please THEN don't tell me that. I was still the rising star. Coming up fast. Success cascading fireworks in my night sky. The guttered stick would fall to earth.

Spike said, 'John, you've got a Jekyll and Hyde personality. After a couple of drinks it's as though someone has pulled a switch inside you.' But he accepted me, always. He wrote to me when I was in a mental hospital. He tolerated me when I turned up drunk. He lent me money when I was broke. Looking back, looking forwards, I did not see any of that coming. It could only get better…

I was staying at St Ives in Cornwall. I had discovered the Artists Colony, on whose recommendation I know not, and decided to write a major play for the stage while living off repeats for The Frankie Howerd Radio Show which were pouring in at £13 a week. One day as the sun shone on the glistening waters of the harbour and the seagulls wheeled and caawed like a bad tempered theatre audience, I received a telegram to phone Spike at his office. I asked the beatnik who was living in the public phone box if I could possibly make a call. He seemed surprised but not too put out.

'Yeah, sure man. I'll go for a walk.'

I got on the phone to the office and was put through to Spike.

Spike: Hello, young John! What are you doing in Cornwall?

Me: I'm writing a play, Spike.

Spike: What's it about?

Me: Well, a man arrives at a village, pushing a wheelbarrow in which he has a lot of files. He books a room and starts to interview women. He is looking for his long lost sweetheart, Molly Potts, from whom he was separated during the war. It has been his quest to find her after all these years and he has abandoned everything to devote himself to this task. He interviews someone he believes to be her… but then to accept this as fact would mean giving up his search, his filing system, his journey which has become his life. So he finds a way to deny her and move on…

Spike: Do you think there's a Goon Show in it?

Me: Probably not.

It was arranged that I would put my play aside and return to London to write a Goon Show with Spike. The play was never finished but we would write The Spon Plague for the BBC.

The character in the unfinished play was, I can now see, based on Spike, with a multitude of box files attempting to create order in a chaotic world. Yes, Spike, who in his den above the greengrocers in Shepherd's Bush would pull one file after another from the shelves with fluttering paperwork escaping, the phone ringing and knocks on the door and someone he loved spending spending and a house and children which he tried to live in with her but he could only grasp properly through the files. Hope to control. To order UNTIL TOO MUCH he collapsed and returned to the nursing home for another 72-hour sleep. The files went with him when we moved offices to Kensington, then to Bayswater. He divorced his wife and found another but kept the files and adjusted his life through them. His life was in the box files. He stuffed in lawyers' fee accounts, 'New bastards'.

To be fair, from his filing also came much literary output. The sayings and drawings of his children. The recollections and photographs of war comrades. Letters from parents. Scraps of his own childhood. India. Was there an India file? Spike was methodical. Not crazy, zany Spike, but a man who reached into his history with love, to rescue what he could. His heart shone through those files. But there was a dark shelf in those early days where he struggled with banks, bank managers, household bills and Harrods and lawyers and tax-collectors to create room – space and time to write. Sometimes the filing system won.

There were good days. And very good days. A good day would be to enter Spike's office and find him conducting with a baton the music from a gramophone. Some classical piece. Vivaldi's *The Four Seasons*. Did it need conducting? Holst's *The Planets*. They sounded better when Spike stood conducting the gramophone as the record turned. He never missed a beat. Though he found time to brush his hair back, extravagantly. The expressions on his face would have warmed an orchestra. He could have filled the Albert Hall. But there was only me waiting for him to stop, for the record to finish, so that we might start writing.

'Come in, John!'

Another time might find him painting in oils. He admired Van Gogh and his work had that influence and his mind certainly did. Exultation. Depression. A very good day would finding him conducting the gramophone with a paint brush. Dear Spike. When he laughed... when we laughed we had to push the furniture back to make room. 'We know John's in with him'. Downstairs would say. Because our laughter could be heard throughout the building. If laughter keeps you healthy then some days we were supermen.

There was a man who walked down St Ives High Street with a Vacant To Let expression. But suddenly he would burst out laughing and then as suddenly stop. Was it a neurological trigger, a chemical fusion? Or had he shared the genius of the Gods and known himself to be immortal for those seconds? And then nothing.

Were we so different?

Shepherd's Bush Green. An optimistic title for a beleagured piece of ground that no-one but a meths-drinking alcoholic would fight over. A soggy place surrounded by rushes of traffic, a brick toilet at one end then for fifties cottaging and an underground toilet at the other, since converted into a snooker club. The brick toilet has gone too and no blue plaque announcing 'Here Wilfred Brambell was arrested.' Litter blows from one end to the other. Sometimes a funfair would appear on the green. Trucks, mud, diesel engines and cables, and the garish lights of stalls and amusements. Mechanical music and bumping cars. Roundabouts and candy floss. I suppose someone must have enjoyed themselves there. It could not have been a place where only sex deviations were dreamt of though when the trucks were cleared and the fair was gone it was surprising not to see the corpses of half a dozen half-dressed tarts lying on the grass limbs akimbo in deathly pose. The hangman was employed those days and judges donning black caps had reason to thank Shepherd's Bush for their employment.

On a clear and sunny day the sound of Spike blowing his trumpet could be heard on The Green. And shop workers sitting huddled on benches chewing sandwiches could have looked across the road and seen him at the window. He would have waved, and they waved back. We were all survivors who had won the war and had to pay for it now – waiting for the Sixties and Flower Power to arrive. We were still obedient to our masters then, the Establishment. The Tories were back. My God, we needed The Goons. *Round The Horn* was not enough. We lived on humour – radio humour – and funny voices, impressions of our favourite Goon characters, at bring-a-bottle parties. Radio kept us going.

Educating Archie penned brilliantly by Eric Sykes meant Peter Brough could do a ventriloquist act on radio and move his lips as much as he liked. Frankie Howerd was fun. I used to do impressions of him, 'Ah, just get meself comfy. No, don't laugh Madam. She might have put her teeth in before she came out for the evening. That's a nice handbag. Where did you get that? Has your wife got one too? So I went to the dentists. Oh. Ah…' Eric wrote monologues that I improvised upon as a schoolboy. Then Ray and Alan (Simpson and Galton) and *Hancock's Half-Hour*. Stalwart. Suffering Britain in Tony Hancock personified, making the best of it. Muir And Norden. *Take it From Here. Oh Ron! Oh Eff*. The Glums.

It was radio, radio, radio. Catch phrases and funny voices. You could laugh for nothing even if money was tight. TV was knocking on the door, the unruly child would enter soon, but radio was still in it's heyday. The anarchy of the Goons spoke to our Spirit. With the other officer cadets at Sandhurst I would rush from the dining rooms for the weekly fix of Major Bloodnok, Eccles, and Grytpype Thynne. And Min and Henry Bannister. The invisible world of words, radio, worked its magic. The spell was cast. And the hard lumpen authoritarian greyness of Fifties Britain, with all it's fixtures and fittings would soon be packed away in the box marked HISTORY. I heard the music. I threw away my uniform and joined the band. It was hardly a conscious decision, leaving Sandhurst. Simply put, 'There must be something else, out there.' There was, and I went out to find it. Through the gates of the RMA for the last time…

Spon Plague Plot: Moriaty models in the nude for a pill that Grytpype Thynne invents to cure a disease that no-one has ever yet caught, calling it the Spon Plague. It's symptoms are bare knees and when Neddy Seagoon rolls up his trousers…

NED: Ahhhhhhh – I've got the Spon!

The Ministry of Health after thirty years came up with the answer – immunising everyone with long woollen underpants. But long woollen underpants covering bare knees was a symptom of another disease invented by Grytpype, called the Quodge...

The day came to record *Spon Plague* at the Camden Theatre. Well, I mean, it should have been an unforgettable experience to a young writer... his first Goon Show! (I only wrote two with Spike). But I don't remember anything except that the audience were sitting south of the stage and that could be an illusion because I didn't bring a compass. I sought the help of a Deep Hypnotist to bring back this golden event...

Hypnotist: Relax, Mr Antrobus. Relax. I'm counting you back through the years.

Me: Start at 1970, please. I'm paying.

Hypnotist: Relax. So... when did you go to the theatre? What time of day?

Me: Early afternoon. I think. Well, for the read through.

Hypnotist: As you approach the theatre. Imagine you are... Is it raining?

Me: No, but the sky's leaking.

Hypnotist: Good. You are in the theatre. You are saying hello to everybody. You say hello to Peter Sellers. What does he reply?

Me: Hello, Johnny.

Hypnotist: Good. You say hello to Harry Secombe. What does he reply?

Me: Hello, Neddy! Stand well back to avoid falling into conversation! Thank you!

Hypnotist: Good. You say hello to Spike Milligan. What does he reply?

Me: We'll never get these sound effects right.

Hypnotist: I want you to touch something. A fabric. What was Spike wearing?

Me: A tent.

Hypnotist: Touch it. What does it feel like.

Me: Canvas. Spike liked to live under canvas.

Hypnotist: Good. What is Peter Sellers wearing?

Me: The suit. The Goons saved up for one and it was Peter's turn to wear it. He had it for the first twelve years.

Hypnotist: How was Harry Secombe dressed?

Me: With difficulty. It was before they had Oxfam shops. He used to go up to people in the street and say how much do you want for that pullover? He didn't know you could buy clothes in shops. He thought they were issued by the Quarter Master Sergeant and he didn't know where he lived. He had the most difficulty adjusting to Civvy Street. He kept asking for the NAAFI…

Hypnotist: So you're talking to Harry Secombe, good…

Me: I told him the war was over and he asked me who won. I tell him Wales and he was ever so grateful.

Hypnotist: Excellent. Then what's happening next?

Me: We have a read through. It goes well. Everyone laughs a lot. Then Peter says, 'Is it funny?' and Spike says, 'I bloody well hope so.' And nobody talks to each other for half an hour… Then we have a run-through onstage and the band is laughing so everyone gets their confidence back.

Hypnotist: Go on, go on…

Me: Then we had a tea break and Max Geldray tried to sell me a watch.

Hypnotist: Did it keep good time?

Me: No, but he gave me a free calendar.

Hypnotist: And then what is happening? Now?

Me: The show is going to start. Spike is playing the piano and the audience is coming in. Harry says, 'Thank God Spike's not playing the Warsaw Concerto tonight, that's always a bad sign.' Then the show starts and I'm sitting in the audience and I laugh louder than anybody else. And then it's over.

Hypnotist: Is everybody happy?

Me: Yes, it's like they've driven a bus back to Mitcham Garage and gone off duty. Job done, know what I mean?

The alarm clock rattled on the hypnotist's desk and I paid him £50 in cash which he put in a biscuit tin. He showed me the door.

'Do you like it?'

'Yes, it's a very nice door. Goodnight.'

I stepped out into Marylebone High Street.

It was raining and I knew the case wasn't getting any easier. The hypnotist was obviously a fraud. Perhaps he did know where the bodies were buried. I turned up the collar of my Burberry and walked down the wet glistening pavement, puddles reflecting street lights and traffic wooshing past, each car its own world. I sensed that I was being trailed. I quickened my pace and as I turned a corner I saw that it was a man pushing a gas stove who was following me. He too quickened. I turned to confront him as he came after me. The figure stopped, bent over the gas stove and removed something. He stood up and the next moment a strange pancake shaped object was winging towards my face. In an instant I knew Spike was the Catford Cake-mix Chucker... My friend, co-writer, had turned Beast, living out his own fantasies.

There was a junk shop on The Green, or had it slipped in memory down the Goldhawk Road? Spike liked to visit such places and rummage round for treasures. We would take a break from work and pop into this sun-struck establishment to be met by the proprieter in a cloth cap. 'Hello, mate.'
        'Hello, mate,' said Spike.
        'Hello, mate,' I echoed.
        'Anything out the back?' asked Spike.
        'Oh, it's all out there, mate. Go and have a look, mate. Are you looking for a particular something? Are you, mate?'
        'Maybe a set of mirrors.'
        'Ah.'
        'Ah, what?'
        'Ah, mate.'
        We went out the back and I marvelled how the sun always shone here. It was on Shepherd's Bush Green, yes, and across the road the merry brickwork of the cottaging toilet glowed in the light of that ever present day, waiting for sunset, while the police planned that night's entrapment at the local cop-shop.

'You got the big chopper, Forty Nine, so you'll be the first in.'
        'Right, Inspector.'
        'Wriggle it around a bit and see if you get any offers. But don't make the first move, or you'll spoil it.'

'Right, Inspector.'

'That's what Ernie did. We had to send him down to Ealing for a fresh start.'

Old Mate puffed and blew as he helped Spike move pieces of dusty furniture in the back of the shop.

'I been looking for that, mate,' he said. 'It's a steam iron. Or it will be when it's been adapted.'

Spike wouldn't give up. 'Do you think there's a set of mirrors in here?'

'You can think what you like, mate. If you want to think about a set of mirrors, mate, you go ahead… mate.'

'Right, mate,' said Spike. 'Who's writing this scene?'

'Both of us,' I said.

'Right,' said Spike. 'Keep going and we'll get an ending.'

Spike and the wheezing Old Mate heaved the wardrobe aside. There stood another Old Mate, an identical copy though he had a walrush moustache.

'Hello, mate,' said Old Mate

'Hello, mate,' said Walrush.

'What are you doing there mate, behind that there wardrobe, mate?' said Old Mate. 'I thought you'd gone to Austragglia.'

'No, mate, I didn't go to Austragglia. I got trapped behind this wardrobe when we moved it last time, mate.'

'Did you call out for help, mate.'

'No, mate. It takes a brilliant brain to think of things like that. Lucky I had me sandwiches, mate, so I was orlright… mate.

'Oh, mate.'

'Oh, mate.'

'Help me put the wardrobe back,' said Spike.

They replaced the wardrobe in front of the Walrush Mate.

Spike and I strolled back to the office, conversing. 'That was a nicely written scene, John.'

'It was from an original sketch by Dave Freeman.'

'Credit where credit's due. Pity about the set of mirrors though. Let's write them in.'

So we did.

Spike carefully carried the newly written walnut-framed set of mirrors up the narrow staircase over the greengrocer's shop. We passed various photographs and posters on the way and a framed cheque for a million pounds which bore the instructions underneath, 'In case of bankruptcy, break glass and cash cheque immediately'.

Spike put the set of mirrors down on his desk. He fetched a duster and squirted the wooden frames with Pledge, polishing them up nicely.

'Not bad for ten bob,' he said.

We wrote our days, we wrote our lives in Shepherd's Bush. We wrote laughter and money and friendship, Ray Galton and Alan Simpson, Eric Sykes, Johnny Speight, Spike and I and others who might tell this tale their own way. It came time to go. We were moving up in the world, to High Street Kensington, opposite Kensington Palace Gardens where new offices were rented. Goodbye, Shepherd's Bush. We left our innocence there. We were beginning to sense our importance. We were going to kick the rest of the Fifties up the arse and start a New Decade. The Troggs would sing, 'Here Comes The Night'. I didn't know they were singing my song.

Spike began to see dark shapes. Like Van Gogh's crows they filled his sky. His paintings looked like Van Gogh's. And even he looked like Van Gogh. Vincent and Spike. Spike still had both ears so he was ahead of the game. His office door was more often locked and even I did not knock, being otherwise employed. I would meet him occasionally in the corridor or the reception area. His face was stubbled and gaunt but he would take the trouble to ask how I was doing.

'Put your money into things of value,' he would advise me. 'Then you will have the pleasure of ownership and something to fall back on if you need cash.'

But I laughed off his advice and spent rivers of money getting pissed. I could only see it getting better and I was wrong. The day of reckoning would come but meanwhile I had become an atheist and would even taunt God. Had not Bernard Shaw stood on a lecture platform and challenged, 'If there be an all powerful God strike me down with lightning!' But GBS did not play golf so he was playing it safe.

I asked Spike once, 'Do you believe in God?'

'Yes' he replied. 'But he's left too much for me to do. He shouldn't have rested on the Seventh Day. He'd have done better to finish His Creation and then take his family for a fortnight's holiday in Torremolinos.'

Spike was trying to fill in for God. That was part of the problem. It was too much for any man…

And Spike said to God, 'I can't save humanity on my own. I give up.'

And God replied, 'You've never been the same since you played Coventry.'

And Spike said, 'A prophet is without honour in his own country and couldn't get a laugh in Coventry even if he tried.'

And God replied, 'Harry Secombe did with his shaving routine.'

And it came to pass that God sent Spike to Harrods to enquire about the lawn mower – which had not been repaired for many a moon – and to cry out against the Service Department and it's wickedness.

And Spike did rail mightily against the Manager of the Service Department who had not taken his telephone calls but used a spotty youth to hide behind, who had answered the telephone previously saying, 'We're waiting for a spare part to come from Germany, Mr Milligan.'

'But my lawn mower is Made In Britain,' Spike had replied, not without pride. And the Spotty Youth had answered thus. 'That is very patriotic, sir.'

And Spike had demanded of the spotty quavering voice, 'Why are we waiting for a spare part to come from Germany when my machine is made in England?'

'I give up,' saith Spotty. 'Next question, please.'

Immediately Spike had rushed from his building and hailed a cab to take him hence to Harrods. For he was in a mighty rage and was ready to save England from mediocrity and his lawn in North Finchley from unkemptness.

And God said to Spike in the taxi, 'Smite hard the foe. For by their unbelieving do they mock me.'

Thus Spike stood before the Service Manager in Harrods Lower Floor to repeat his question. The Spotty Youth lay bleeding at his feet but that was normal for he was on a lunch break.

'Why? Why? Why are we waiting for a spare part from Germany when my machine is Made In Britain?' cried out Spike.

And the manager replied 'There has been a misapprehension, Mr Milligan. The spare part is for the van that will carry your well serviced lawn mower back to Finchley. We regret the misunderstanding, sir.'

And Spike, being of good nature, was reconciled to Harrods and to the Manager of the Service Department. And to the Spotty Youth who lay bleeding Spike sang this lament:

> A poor young Harrods Assistant Trainee Manager lay dying,
> Out on the lone prairie,
> His thin legs so bare,
> Lay with him there,
> And they sang in harmony…
> Take my false teeth back to Ireland
> And give them to Mother McCree
> For a poor young Harrods Assistant Trainee Manager's last wish is…
> Oh please wash the dishes,
> That drove me away from you!

And the Spotty Youth was healed by the tender sentiment of Spike's lament and he rose from the floor, full of hope. And Spike hit him.

The Manager by way of recompense offered to give Spike a lift back to Finchley with the lawn mower in the Harrods electric van.

'We just have to stop off with another delivery sir, on the way. A piano. A Bechstein, so you'll be in good company.'

And Spike agreed to make peace and to travel with the Bechstein, demanding only a ten per cent discount on July's bill and a box of fine wines.

Thus did Spike set off from Harrods in the Van Electric, destination Finchley, stopping off only once in Uzbekistan where the piano was to be delivered to a tribal chief who wished to emulate Fats Waller, playing ragtime.

It was some time before Spike returned to the office in High Street Kensington from which had issued forth to do the Mighty work of God in Harrods which had taken him to Uzbekistan where he was much better received than in Coventry. Possibly because he had tried out Harry Secombe's shaving routine on the locals.

But another version of Spike's absence was that he had gone back to The Clinic and the clanging dustbin lids. Eric Sykes took over writing The Goon Shows until Spike returned one day, pale and composed. The black shapes that had joined up and become Spike's darkest night had dissolved and he threw himself back into work on The Goons. His office door was unlocked and there was laughter in the land. And great was the rejoicing.

Larry Stephens died of a heart attack. He was a handsome man, affable and talented. I can't remember that he blew raspberries or spoke in funny voices or knocked on the door then lay flat in the corridor and when the door was opened asked if this was an undertakers. Perhaps being quiet brought something that Spike needed. Indeed that must have been the case or Spike would have written alone and not halved the fee. Larry came and went in Spike's life. Then he was gone forever.

In our new offices, opposite the entrance, there was a blackboard and upon it written in chalk were the writers' names and their current assignments, rather as if we were in an ops room of Bomber Command and Beryl Vertue, agent supremo, was pushing models around on a model table saying, 'Galton and Simpson returning from Pinewood Studios. Eric Sykes approaching ATV. John Antrobus and Johnny Speight stuck in The Goat And Boots…'

I came back to the office late afternoon, slightly sozzled. I could see no point in this board, drunk or sober, nor can I still. I picked up a piece of chalk and rubbed out Larry's assignment and wrote, R.I.P. I thought it was funny then. Now I don't think it's so funny. God bless you, Larry.

Spike went to the funeral. He told me later that he had found a woman to be sexually aroused who was close to Larry... 'How can they be like that on such an occasion?'

'Sex and death,' I said. 'Anyway it takes two to tango, doesn't it?'

Spike stared at me. Was I shifting the blame on to him for something he may have done? He could not bear to be in the wrong.

'They're meant to be the better sex,' he said, as if it were irrefutable.

Shepherd's Bush was Upstairs Downstairs and so were the next set of offices across the park in Bayswater where ALS would eventually settle, but in High Street Ken we were Ground Floor Sideways. There were no Upstairs People to shout Downstairs and no Downstairs People to come up with tea or more importantly contracts. We would shout sideways to each other and there were Further Down The Corridor And Round The Corner People, of which I was one. My own office I had there and next door was Johnny Speight. And Brad Ashton was down the end honing jokes for Bob Monkhouse. We all paid our rent and ten per cent and so did the Big Boys, the company directors.

According to Spike the agency was envisioned as a commune but it had all gone pear-shaped Capitalistic because of the others thinking only about money, so he'd lost interest.

We held Writer's Meetings once a week and Spike attended the first one for a few minutes until Johnny Speight asked something like, 'If all the ten per cents add up to more than the salaries, rent and the office charges, where does the excess money go?' Whereupon Spike stalked out and returned to his office, slamming the door, never to return. It was a comment of sorts, though I have not been able to decipher it. Was Spike on the side of The Workers but hopelessly compromised? Or did he want to grind us down into the dust until we arose with bloody revolution in our hearts when he would have said, 'I did it for your own good, lads. You had to see for yourselves how corrupt the system is.' Or did he not enjoy discussing company policy with writers such as me and Johnny who had spent the previous hours in The Goat And Boots discussing Trotsky, spending our ill-gotten gains getting pissed again? One thing for sure. The flag of Communism would not rise outside our premises. We were all on Nice Little Earners as we fiercely debated Socialism. Eric Sykes was the Office Right Winger. Thank God for the Loyal Opposition and his drinks cabinet. Long sessions ensued. Fierce debate. God, how we cared! Nothing was settled, except that we often got drunk, me, Johnny, Ray, Alan, Eric and any visitor drawn into our vortex. The Bright Tomorrow we discussed was invariably Hangover Day.

Spike had little to do with these sessions. He had enough demons to fight without the Demon Drink. And as for the rest of us, Youth was on our side, our metabolisms still strong. In varying degrees we coped with our excesses till age brought wisdom or the doctor said if you don't stop it will kill you. But I was always barmy on drink.

Spike said to me, 'After you've had three or four drinks I can see the change in your eyes. Suddenly I'm talking to someone else.'

He might as well have been talking to a brick wall. A brick wall was what I was going to hit. Meanwhile, ever upwards!

And it came to pass that Spike and John would write a second Goon Show. And it came to be called *The Great Statue Debate*.

Around this time Maggie came through the window one night of a vile basement flat I was renting in Kensington Church Street. I had met her previously at Bungee's Coffee House and found her 18-year-old appearance much to my liking – a dark-eyed, black-haired beatnik in a duffle coat. (She'll probably tell you different, but I know she was never blonde). Maggie comes into my next excursion with Spike, thus the intro.

All sorts of good writing jobs were coming my way. I had a natural flair for scriptwriting, though I was still determined to become a playwright and rather (sadly) looked down upon my easy talents.

Spike: What are you writing these days, John?

Me: It's a play about a man who works for an organisation. He wants to complain about something and is told he must do so through the appropriate channels. But there seems to be no complaints procedure, no complaints department and this is what he really wants to complain about, forgetting why he started…

Spike (*laughing*): Good. Anything else?

Me: Yes. Morecambe and Wise.

Spike: Have you got time to write another Goon Show with me?

Me: Definitely.

Spike: I've promised Harry Secombe I'll go and see him in Coventry. He's topping the bill with his shaving routine.

Me: What did you do when you played Coventry?

Spike: I played the trumpet standing on one leg.

Me: Did they like it?

Spike: They liked the leg. It was the bit they could understand. They've all got legs. A journalist up there – a local man – asked me why I played the trumpet hopping around on one leg? Had the other one been hurt in the war? I said no, my mind had been hurt in the war, that's why I played the trumpet hopping around on one leg. Why use two legs? It's wasteful.

Me: What did you do for an encore?

Spike: I took my sock off and threw it in the audience.

Me: Did they go mad?

Spike: No they went home. Would you like to come up to Coventry for a few days, John? We could stay at the Hotel Leofric and write our show. There'd be no distractions from wives.

Me: I'm not married.

Spike: Well we're not going up till Friday.

Me: OK.

Before we left for Coventry, Spike bought me a book, *From Gandhi To Vinoba*'. 'This book will change your life,' he said. Well, most books did. And every film I went to see. As I've mentioned, I was very impressionable in those days.

And the Good Fairy transported us to the Hotel Leofric and set us down in adjoining rooms. The first evening we had dinner in the dining room.

Spike: Do you like devouring meat, John?

Me: Yes, I like my steak medium rare, Spike.

Spike: Could you look an animal in the eyes and kill it?

Me: No, I'd have to turn the lights off.

Spike: The way half this country makes love. Thinking they're Clark Gable and Jane Russell, though not sure which is which. And saving on the electricity bill, the mean buggers.

Me: Yes, my father used to go round the house taking out the light bulbs. But as we only had gas it didn't make much difference.

Spike: My father in India sought out a guru. A most holy man. He was so holy a light emanated from his being and he was able to read *The Madras Times* at midnight.

Me: What, your father?

Spike: Yes.

Me: Up a mountain, was he? This holy man?

Pike: No, they used such people for street lighting in Calcutta. It was cheaper.

Me: Why was your father reading *The Madras Times* in Calcutta?

Spike: It was the fashion. You read *The Madras Times* and wore *The Calcutta Times*.

Me: Ah!

Spike: And curried the *Rangoon Chronicle*.

Me: That makes sense.

Spike: How are you enjoying your gory steak?

Me: Nicely, thanks. The funny thing is, though I love meat, I hate rice pudding.

Spike: Could you kill a rice pudding in anger?

Me: Oh, no.

Spike: That's illogical, John. If you really hated a rice pudding you would eat it to destroy it. And if you truly loved meat you couldn't eat it. I mean, do you feel threatened by that entrecôte steak?

Me: Yes, it looks very dangerous, Excuse me while I finish it off…

I tucked into my succulent steak. I had yet to be converted. Though I was definitely undermined and felt like a slobbering monster, blood drooling down my chin. Of course Spike was a vegetarian though he occasionally ate fish in those days. We laughed a lot at our own jokes. If we did not, it would be a pretty bad sign. It would be like a plumber living in a house with all the taps dripping.

A waiter hurried over to our table.

Waiter: Gentlemen, could you please keep your voices down. There are residents in this dining room trying to sleep.

Spike: That's one of my jokes.

Waiter: Yes, it's unexploded, Spike. I picked it up when you were last up here.

Spike: I don't wish to know that. What year is this wine?

Waiter: What year would you like it to be, sir? We'll write it on the bottle.

Spike: I'm surrounded by comedians. I'm the only one in Coventry who doesn't get a laugh.

Waiter: When I saw you die onstage, I knew I was looking at a very brave man.

Spike: I could have surrendered but I bet Harry Secombe I'd last the week.

We called our second Goon Show *The Great Statue Debate*. The story concerns Parliament being evicted from the House of Commons due to a Housing Act they have just passed and travelling around on a London tram whilst trying to re-frame the legislation to get back in.

We were getting on so well with the script I asked Spike if he would mind if Maggie came up and stayed with me. He said alright so I phoned Maggie and invited her to come up. I explained that I was greatly influenced by a book Spike had given me called *From Gandhi To Vinoba* so I'd book us into a cheap bed and breakfast and we could give the money we saved to the poor. She said no and came up to spend a couple of nights at the Leofric anyway. The honeymoon suite became vacant so Spike moved up there to have more room. *From Gandhi To Vinoba* did not seem to be having the same effect upon him.

Maggie discovered that I had £832 in the bank which greatly surprised her so we bought a house in Whitton and got married and had a baby but not necessarily in that order. Spike came to the wedding at Kensington Registry Office and gave us a beautiful present that got smashed later. I couldn't catch everything that was thown at me.

Connie Speight gave us a puppy that we called Wilf. The dog would grow up to be a CND marcher, adding four legs to the forest of protesters. Wilf's demise was unfortunate. We went away one summer and left the dog at my parent's home in Cumbria. Upon returning we learnt that my father had had it shot.

'You said you'd only be away a week,' my father said, reprovingly, handing me an empty collar and lead. 'It's been over a month. We're not really dog people, Mother and I, are we Trixie?'

Trixie went to make a cake.

I gazed into the unblinking, untroubled blue eyes of my father. 'I had it done by a local farmer,' he said, 'so it won't cost you anything.'

Later in bed, Maggie said, 'I'm glad we didn't leave the baby with him.'

I related the story to Spike and he laughed for a fortnight.

My father met Spike once. I had taken him up to the office and introduced him. Dad was wearing his Royal Artillery tie and they got on really well.

'I imagine this writing game is very unreliable, Mr Milligan,' said my father.

'Yes,' replied Spike. 'I'm trying to get a job as a letter sorter at the Post Office.'

'Ah, there'll always be letters!'

'Well, I write enough of them,' said Spike. 'Are you disappointed that John left the army?'

'Not really. He's got his own life to lead, hasn't he? He must learn by his own decisions.'

We went down the pub. After a few drinks my father confided in Spike.

'I admire you and John. You're doing something different. Don't give up. What did we fight for? A land fit for pensions?'

Spike laughing, said, 'Yes, a land where small minds may safely graze.'

He got on so well with my father that I felt a pang of jealousy. It was like being at their Regimental reunion. And I was Poor Bloody Infantry.

Television was finding it's feet and elbowing out Radio. At ALS the writers were more and more employed writing for The Goggle Box. What came up was this...

'Can we put Goon humour on TV?'

'No,' said Spike. 'It definitely won't work. Goon humour conjures up the imagination and that only radio can do.'

Fair enough.

Peter Sellers decided to go ahead as he had been offered a deal by Associated Rediffusion. So Johnny Speight and I signed on as principal writers though others made significant contributions. Joining the cast to support Sellers were Graham Stark and Kenneth Conner, plus David 'Cockleshell Heroes' Lodge and Valentine Dyall. Johnny Vivian, a short actor, made up the contingent. Thus was born 'IDIOT WEEKLY. PRICE 2p.'

No Spike.

It was a huge success and showing remarkable versatility – not to mention opportunism – Spike climbed aboard and the next series was called 'Fred'.

Spike's talents as writer and performer flourished and the series went from strength to strength, spawning, 'Son Of Fred'. In the rather Stalinist writing of Show Biz history and it's presentation on TV and Radio I have not heard mention of Spike's initial reluctance to transform his wonderful humour to TV, but this Revisionist text notes it.

Spike's favourite sketch in the series was one I wrote for him and he performed it with Pinteresque relish...

He is at home with his wife when two anonymous men call round and take his measurements on the doorstep, telling him that they will let him know. Spike returns to his wife in the lounge.

Spike: He's going to let me know then.

    Wife: Who is?

    Spike: The man wot took my measurements.

    Wife: Wot?

    Spike: Yeah, there was a man wot called round like – and he took me measurements.

    Wife: Where's he from?

    Spike: Oh, he didn't say – no he didn't mention it – I didn't fink to ask him…

    Wife: And you let him take your measurements?

    Spike: Yeah – wot's wrong with that then?

    Wife: A man wot calls round – you don't know where he's from – you don't know who he is – and you let him take your measurements…

    Spike: Wot's wrong wiv that then? There's nothing wrong with my measurements – I got nothink to hide…

    Wife: You don't know wot you got, do you? Mr Jones down the road – they come and took his measurements, didn't they?

    Spike: Did they?

    Wife: Yes, they come and took his measurements… And look wot happened to him.

    Spike: Well, we don't know what happened to him, do we? He disappeared, didn't he? On the way home from work.

    Wife: Yes, the day after they took his measurements…

    Spike: …You never complained the day we got married, when the vicar said to you – Do you take this man, head 18, chest 42, inside leg 28, to be your lawfully wedded husband…

He happens to look out of the window and sees Mr Jones walking down the street. There is a moment of relief, followed by renewed anxiety.

    Spike: It's Mr Jones! They've changed his measurements…

To the Zoo.

We went to Regent's Park Zoo to do outside filming for a sketch – the idea being that while the animals variously went off for a fortnight's holiday, unemployed actors would stand in for them. Dick Lester (we never called him Richard then) was the director, up and coming, very talented, whose most used line was, 'Yes, of course we can do it.'

Graham Stark was supposed to be standing in for a sea lion who had gone to Margate to visit relatives at the aquarium. Graham stood shivering in his striped one-piece bathing suit, at the edge of the pool, gazing mistrustfully at the sea lions.

'Are they dangerous?' he asked the keeper.

'Only if they think you want their food,' said the keeper. 'Don't worry, I'll feed them down the other end.'

So Starkers slipped into the pool – we always gave him the dangerous jobs to show him how much we loved him – and Richard Lester was ready to shoot.

'Action!' shouted Dick.

'What action?' demanded Starkers.

'Can you pretend to eat a raw sprat?'

'You've got to be joking,' spluttered Starkers. 'For Christ's sake, shoot. I'm freezing in here!'

Next Valentine Dyall got into the vultures cage. Val was wearing a black cloak which he spread out as he perched next to a large-ominous looking, hood-eyed vulture. Val was frightened. He need not have worried, for the vulture warily moved along the perch away from the actor who had once played Hamlet at the Old Vic. Valentine looked like death warmed up (as usual) but the vulture was not attracted by the dish of the day.

Spike got into the monkey cage and amazed the other primates therein with his impressions. He so much passed for one of them that a mother monkey tried to feed him. He accepted the banana in good spirit. Spike was having a good time until one of the young males started masturbating, when he hurriedly left the cage.

Peter Sellers rolled up a trouser and stood on one leg in the flamingo enclosure. He did not look at all like a flamingo but he did look like a hungry unemployed actor grasping at a once in a lifetime chance of stardom.

A jolly good day was had by all. It was only when we were leaving that we remembered to go back and take Valentine Dyall out of the vultures cage. 'It was not a problem,' he said. 'I knew you'd be back. I had *Sporting Life* on me. I think I've found a winner for the 3.30 at Newbury.'

Back To The Zoo. Spike was to pay another visit to Regent's Park Zoo, but under far less happy circumstances. It concerned a goldfish and I was deeply involved. Spike came into my office one morning and noticed a solitary goldfish floating near the top of a fish tank on the window still. There had been three and, despite my aerating the tank, two of them had come to the surface and after a few desolatory tail flicks gone belly up. I had spooned them out and thrown them in the waste paper basket. I was not a goldfish person, nor tropical fish, I hadn't got into it and created a beautiful underwater world. Somebody else had parked the tank upon me as they were homeless. They did not want to walk round the streets with three goldfish visiting accommodation agencies because in those days landlords were very prejudiced, particularly against tropical fish. In Paddington you would often see a notice in the window of a seedy rooming house, 'ROOM TO LET. NO TROPICAL FISH.'

Spike stood in the doorway, staring across the room.
>   Spike: That fish isn't very well, John.
>   Me: I know. I'm looking after them for David.
>   Spike: Them?
>   Me: Well, there were three. But two died.
>   Spike: Have you been feeding them?
>   Me: Yes. That could be the problem.
There was a scum of bread crumbs on the surface of the water, stirred by a sluggish swish of the occupant's tail. Spike stepped across the room and peered into the murky tank.
>   Spike: All the plants have died too.
>   Me: I know. It's depressing. That's why I sit facing the door. I try not to think about it.
>   Spike: Have you tried changing the water?
>   Me: What, into wine?

Spike: That fish is lonely. We must do something.

Me: Yes, Spike.

Spike: It's got no incentive to live. I know how it feels. It's in a dead environment. Even the snails are dead.

Me: Are they?

Spike: The shells are empty.

Me: Is that a sign? Where have they gone?

Spike: To Harrods. I don't know, John. All I know is that all life is sacred.

Spike left the office. I went down the pub with Johnny Speight. When I returned to my office a couple of hours later I saw that the fish was missing...

Then Beryl Vertue told me, 'Spike has taken your goldfish in a taxi to London Zoo, John.' I knew he was busy writing a Goon Show and that this represented a major disruption to his day.

Johnny Speight said, 'He's mad.'

As Johnny had been spending two hours in The Goat saloon bar explaining to me why Stalin was justified in moving hundreds of thousands of Russian peasants off their land, terrorising them into subjection to bring about the New Utopia, I could hardly expect him to be concerned about a two-inch, off colour goldfish. History was what mattered to Johnny. Evolution. Its relentless march against the dead state of mind of the masses. The visionary Stalin had to be ruthless to drag the Soviet Union into the twentieth century.

As we chatted the afternoon away, Spike returned. No sign of the goldfish. No empty jam jar.

'What happened, Spike?' I asked, not wanting to upset him.

'They had to put it to sleep,' said Spike. Resignedly he went to his room and shut the door behind him. He knew he had done his best. We, the Mockers, the Damned, Stalinists and Don't Knows, were the losers. Because we never even tried. We didn't lift a finger to save that morsel of fish life. We just talked.

I wanted to recall the recording of the second Goon Show I had worked on, about which I was deeply traumatised and decided to revisit my equally deep hypnotist. This was an earlier event, true but it must surface whenever I was able to face it. Surely it should have been a happy event? What could have gone wrong at the Camden Theatre that April Sunday in 1954?

On the way to Marylebone High Street to visit Professor Wretch, to give him a name, I found myself turning up a side alley, a dark and dismal mews where I knew resided two old friends of Spike, Grim and Nonny Towelrail. My footsteps ceased at their green flaked door and I applied myself to the knocker. I wanted information.

Within the sound reverberated.

Nonny: There's somebody at the door, Grim.

Grim: Oh, dear, Nonny. It must be someone else.

Nonny: What do you mean? Someone else?

Grim: Well, it's not us this time, is it? I've just counted us and we're both here.

Nonny: It would be raining if we were outside.

Grim: It's raining inside, Nonny. It costs extra. That way we don't have to water the aspidistra.

FX: KNOCK ON DOOR.

Grim: There he goes again. Listen to that crazy rhythm, buddy!

Nonny: Yes, it's driving me insane!

It was a fruitless visit. I knew, or suspected, that Grim and Nonny Towelrail were supplying Spike with the mysterious cake mix which he was so deftly removing from his gas oven and hurling through the air at the unwary – perhaps those he hated or even imagined had been in the audience the week he played Coventry. But then, why me? I had not been in that audience at Coventry. It was strange however that Spike Milligan had invited me to that city to write with him *The Great Statue Debate* about which even now I was visiting Professor Wretch to get total recall of the recording.

I need not have bothered. When I reached his premises, breathless, five minutes late, I could see there was nobody at home, nor likely to be. There was a cardboard notice stuck in the bare window ROOMS TO LET. DEFINITELY NO TROPICAL FISH.

The whole trip was worse than a waste of time. When I turned I noticed across the street in the shadow of a shop doorway – for night had fallen long since and here the sodium street lights fizzled rather than shone, plus the inevitable drizzle further obscured any true observation – who was it? A shadow. A gas stove. A straightening of the shape and drawing back of the arm. The inevitable well-hurled cake mix struck home. This one I had not ducked. It might have been a damp cloth but the taste seeping into my mouth left no doubt. Full marks for the recipe.

'It's all in the mind, folks!' The Goons catchphrase raced through my mind before I blacked out.

Or had I heard the words? A shouted taunt?

I came to in a dry-cleaning establishment.

'That will be £27.50, sir,' said the man, handing me back my suit. I was in QikClean. 'You look like you've had a bit of a shock.'

I paid him. 'Look, I'd rather not get dressed in the shop.'

'That's alright, sir, you can use the street.'

'Thanks.'

I stepped outside and dressed myself as people bustled and shoved past me, eager to get home out of the rain. Out of the day. Into their dreams for which they paid with every working hour.

I was angry. Hurt. Bewildered. I had been seeking enlightenment on the couch of Professor Wretch. Instead I was deeper in the woods, alone with the wind that whispered in a thousand leaves wherever I turned, 'It's all in the mind, folks. It's all in the mind...'

Whitton. A suburban dump. Immune to poetry. An end terrace house where, just married, I moved with Maggie. A place to bring the baby home from the hospital. A garden at the back to put the pram out and me digging, turning rows of sour earth, builders' rubble, planting potatoes, cabbages and kings and her at the window tapping, cup of tea? Throw back to the parental pattern really. I couldn't think of anything better. My father loved the garden, digging, smoking, coughing... resting foot upon the shovel watching the sun set through a Craven A haze. And mother tapping on the window, tea up! Was I really about to replicate that? It was a non-starter for both of us. Mind you the baby wasn't complaining, a beautiful boy we called Nicholas. Whitton was a stalling operation while I was finding my feet, working out with Johnny Speight and George Bernard Shaw, Trotsky, Sartre and Camus – throw in Jack Karoac's *On The Road* – where I was heading... If you'd told me Friern Barnet locked ward, I'd have thought you were the mad one.

We'd have parties in each other's houses where the debate on the New World Order would continue. We would bring our babies and park them in corners and with our wives would laugh and eat and drink until the cows came home. Lots of show biz chat as well. Stories. Jokes. At Ray and Tonia Galton's house in Twickenham I took to toasting him and throwing his fine glasses into the fireplace as the Russians are known to do. When he protested, I accused him of having a bourgeois regard for property so he joined in but set aside his good glasses the next time I came, though we never got down to jam jars. Johnny Speight would talk up a good revolution but he enjoyed a show biz lifestyle with his pretty wife, Connie. My theme, coming from Whitton, was that marriage was a bourgeois institution and that I believed in free love (I'd got that far). Then we'll all go home, each with our respective wives, so you could say not much happened.

Spike was against the Establishment but of the opinion that whatever you put in its place would be equally corrupt because the human race was awful, a lost cause. Having said which he could be friendly and supportive to individual members of our species as long as they didn't remind him of the fact. I mean he wasn't a bird watcher who preferred animals to human beings. He was among us, suffering. Were his political opinions Right or Left? Left. Anarchic. And on Thursdays Fascist. He did not hold any particular party line. He could be passionately for a cause like CND. I never knew him to turn against any individual because of his or her colour race or creed and he always showed respect for anyone's achievement and sympathy for their suffering. But he could make a general comment that I can only describe as bigoted. Once he had formed an opinion he found it hard or impossible to admit to being wrong and would rather lay another opinion on top of it and live the paradox. You might come across all sorts of ideas and opinions in the Pandora's Box of Spike's mind. He has been such a public man, living out the best and the worst of himself, where others would shelter behind their smiles, that surely we can forgive Spike for showing us the dark side of his nature as well. I can.

There is no need to whitewash Spike. Do we have to have our heroes flawless? And our bad guys without a redeeming feature? If so we separate ourselves from our own humanity. Did Spike ever say anything that stuck in my mind or summed him up? Perhaps this, 'Children don't grow up. They disappear.'

We had a party at Whitton. Spike came and lay on the floor all evening. June said, 'He's annoyed at me because I won't stop buying hats.' She was bareheaded, her dark hair shone in it's thick lustre. 'It's true. I do buy lots of hats. It's true. But not as a revenge. Not out of spite. I love hats.' She smiled wanly.

Spike's head was buried in his arms but we heard him say distinctly enough from carpet level, 'How many hats can she wear at one time? She's got fifty. She doesn't wear fifty. OK, if she wore one, she still wouldn't be wearing 49. So it's makes sense to go around bareheaded. It's only the difference of one hat.'

'How many pairs of socks have you got, Spike?' she demanded.

'I wash my socks. You don't wash your hats, do you? You're not that bloody stupid. Yet.'

And that was all we got out of Spike all evening though he did accept a glass of red wine and at one stage propped himself up on one arm to watch the proceedings. While the rest of us made merry, various people would go over to Spike and ask him, 'Are you alright, Spike?' and he would nod wearily and sip his wine and maybe accept a refill. When it was time to go, he did deliver one parting shot after June had said thanks for having us…

'My mother used to mend my socks. Now if I get a hole in them, I'm expected to throw them away.'

'You never throw your socks away, Spike,' retorted June, spiritedly. 'You send them to Australia for your mother to mend.'

At least they were talking when they left which was an improvement on how they arrived. Put it down to good company. Later that night I got a phone call from someone.

'Did we leave our baby behind your settee?'

'Hang on, I'll go and have a look.'

I trooped downstairs and looked behind the settee, then went back to the phone.

'Yes, he's alright. His blanket's covered in fag ash but he's fast asleep.'

'In that case can we come back for him in the morning?'

'Certainly.'

Somewhere in the middle of Harrods she broke down and started crying. The assistant fetched a chair and called the floor manager over.

'I'm sorry,' she said. 'I don't know what came over me.'

'Don't worry, madam. You're not the first, believe me. We had three in Bed Linens last week. It's coming up to Christmas that does it.'

'So sorry…'

'Not at all, madam. Kindly accept this linen hankerchief, embossed, as a token of our regard for your custom.'

'Thank-you,' she replied. 'I'm so… your kindness…' And she broke down into sobs.

'Let it all out, madam. Have a good cry. Nigel, go and bring madam a glass of water.'

'Right, Mr Sampson. Shall I fetch the bottle of aspirin?'

'Yes, I'll sign the chit later.'

Nigel pursed his lips and hurried off through Handbags.

'I don't know why he has to walk like that,' said the floor manager.

She smiled through her tears and dabbed her eyes with the embossed linen hankerchief.

'I noticed that Madam is a Joint Gold Card Account Holder. Would you like me to phone the other signature on your behalf?'

'My husband?'

'We don't enquire. You'd be surprised at some of our joint accounts, madam. If the *News of the World* got hold of the details, it would shake the Kingdom.'

She felt better, listening to the floor manager prattling on, and stood up.

'No, don't phone my husband. I'm sure he's far too busy to come and collect me. Can you direct me to millinery?'

'Third floor, madam. Up the escalator.'

She walked off briskly, resolved not to let go again and be caught unawares… over what? Panic. For what? She didn't understand.

Nigel came back with a glass of water and the aspirin. 'Oh, she's pushed off, has she? Made a complete recovery? You have restored a happy shopper, Mr Sampson.'

'Yes, Mr Whiticomb. Learn from my wiles.'

Nigel took the aspirin with a sip of water then put the chair away. He wondered if he dare steal another pair of ladies shoes today.

She was wrong though. He had been thinking of her. His heart was heavy and he would have welcomed the opportunity to go to Harrods and rescue her from Ladies Shoes and take her home and comfort her.

But she had been too brave. Or perhaps not brave enough to trust that he would come.

Like ships they passed in their night. And the darkness deepened.

Maggie and I (and Nicholas) moved to Clarendon Street in Pimlico. The Whitton residence was sold, our furniture placed in storage, and we now lived in style in a beautiful furnished house.

Spike came to dinner. He said, 'Don't pay rent. You're throwing money away. It won't always be coming in like it is now.' But I could not hear what he was saying. I was doing so well, writing films like *Idol On Parade* for Anthony Newley, after contributing to the first Carry On film, *Carry On Sergeant*. It was money for old rope. It could only get better. Maggie agreed. She was not yet twenty-one and I was still considered the Boy Wonder at twenty-six years old.

The night Spike came to dinner we sat in a charming dining room and we were served dinner by the resident maid. It was a matter of keeping your nerve. The wine was served in fine glasses, not jam jars, and as Ray Galton was not paying for the breakages, they were not being hurled into the fireplace. It was a civilised evening, pleasant, cultured and rare. Spike raved about a Sidney Nolan painting hanging on the wall and decided to have his own 'Nolan' period the next time he visited his mother in Australia.

Our guest had come on his own for he and June had at last split up and Spike was initiating THE DIVORCE – which still seemed such a big deal in those days with adultery having to be proved by one party against another and the steady employment of sad detectives in grey macs photographing couples caught *in flagrante*, sometimes by mutual arrangement. I did not know the details of Spike's divorce, except that like all divorces it was painful, and that he was determined to keep custody of the children, rarely granted to the father in those days. He was sad rather than bitter that night. 'I still love her,' he said. 'But we can't live together.'

'Have you closed your joint account at Harrods?' I asked.

'Yes,' said Spike, keeping a straight face. 'But it wasn't easy.'

I went with Peter Sellers to Muswell Hill. He lived there with his wife, Anne. We bumped into an estate agent he knew, Alf Slynne.

Peter said, 'This is John Antrobus.'

Alf Slynne's eyes widened. 'I nearly married your mother,' he said.

I stared at the balding bespectacled gentleman in front of me. Yes, my mother had told me, 'I could have married Alf Slynne but I decided to wait for your dad to get back from India.'

'I could have been your father,' said Alf, standing on the pavement, staring at me in wonder. I didn't quite see how. I would have been someone else.

'It was a close shave,' said Alf. He was questioning my very existence. Peter enjoyed every moment of the encounter. When we drove off in his car he repeated in perfect mimicry, 'I could have been your father,' then giggled all the way home.

He kept repeating it to Anne, 'I could have been your father,' till she got bored. The funny thing is when Peter said it, he looked like Alf Slynne. To think, he could have been my father…

Peter was very superstitious.

We are on set and Peter says, 'I'll not work with that man. He's wearing purple socks.'

The lighting gaffer, for such he was, says 'Buy me a new pair of socks and I'll change 'em, guv'ner.'

So Peter sends the running boy out to buy him three pairs of socks and everybody's happy. Until Graham Stark, who has the ear of Sellers, says, 'Did you see the veins on his legs? They're more purple than his socks. How about having them stripped out?'

I asked Peter Sellers, 'Why do you fear purple?'

'It's the colour of death,' he replied.

And I said, 'Why do you fear death? Aren't you talking to people the other side?'

Peter considered this. 'Yes,' he said. 'I have spoken to The Departed. But they're all so boring. We're better off here, Johnny. There's one spirit though – Dan Leno, who was a famous music-hall comedian. He's my guardian angel. He told me, don't come up here. Don't be in any hurry, he said. There's an end to suffering up here, that's true, but there's nothing left to laugh at.'

Spike could see the black shapes and sometimes Peter would tease him.

'Do you fear mortality, Spike?'

'No, I fear immortality,' replied Spike. In those days he loved the pill that blanked him out and gave him a three-day sleep in the Finchley clinic. It was as close to oblivion as he could get.

PART II

TO THE PUZZLE FACTORY

'We're sending you home, Mr Antrobus.'
'Why? Am I better?'
'No, but you're having a bad influence on
  the other patients.'

Leave the Lights On, Nurse
John Antrobus

'Where is Spike Milligan?'

When I was born I could understand many languages. It was some time before this knowledge faded like the memory of a dream. I could hear people speaking English and I tried to answer but all I did was dribble, drool and burp. Occasionally someone would stoop over my cot, peer into my eyes and say, 'Who's a lovely boy' and I would want to converse but all I could do was kick my legs and if they picked me up, be sick on their shoulder.

For months – long after all knowledge of other languages had gone – and worse the memory that I had lost this knowledge – I retained absolute clarity in English. I hoped to master the motor necessities of speaking while I still knew all the words – so many of them – so rich was this language I inhabited of Shakespeare and the King James bible.

Once my eyes focused I could also read. The first thing I read was the label under the hood of my pram, Made In Bradford. Where was Bradford?

My inner language comprehension was fading fast – coming and going – I had arrived complete, ONE with the whole damn thing or serene if you like, but there was one question I wanted to put to my custodians, parents as I later learned to call them, one question that itself was fading but came back once with startling clarity, 'Where is Spike Milligan?'

Then it dissolved and was gone and when I met him years later, I had of course forgotten that I was looking for him. All language faded. I was being taught anew. All I really needed to learn was how to use this newfangled body in which I had arrived but they thought I was part of the packaging – part of the wiring – something that switched on when everything else was working. It was so frustrating. But then I would eventually forget I was frustrated and just feel lost and alienated. And that's pretty well how it stayed for the next twenty-one years until I met Spike when something clicked. But if you had told me I had been looking for him all this time, I would have thought you crazy. You know there are no coincidences, don't you?

'Don't talk about sex, politics or religion in front of your mother,' said my father.

As I was only five I asked him, 'What are they, Dad?'

'I'll tell you when you're older, son. But not in front of your mother.'

Dad was a sergeant in the Royal Horse Artillery. We were stationed at Larkhill, School of Gunnery on Salisbury Plain when I was a nipper. On Sunday mornings he would walk me round the stables.

'Oh, aren't the horses big, Dad?'

'It's more the fact that you're small,' replied my father, drawing on the inevitable cigarette, Craven A or Park Drive, all very grown up. But then my father was a grown up. And so were the horses. It was me that was tiny and in my opinion it was going to take me far too long to get big enough to really count in this world. Size mattered. Also in those days children wore short trousers. It was a rite of passage to be allowed your first pair of slacks, years away then. Children were children, a different species and not really expected to grow into adults. To my way of thinking kids would always be kids and the big people who smoked, drank and had all the money would always be like that. I wasn't yet familiar with the idea of people dying and I thought they were born with their clothes on.

Dad would lift me on to the back of one of the giant horses. My eyes would sparkle. 'Hold on to his mane.' I held on. We were in the stalls. We weren't going anywhere but I decided I had begun a long journey.

As we walked home, across the lark-laden fields to Bidolph Road, NCO's quarters – my hand securely tucked in that of my father's – he asked me, 'What would you like to be when you grow up, John?'

'Just like you, Dad.'

'Yes?' Another reflective puff on his cigarette. 'Well, I'm often frightened that I won't ever amount to anything in this world.'

'That's how I want to be, Dad. Frightened that I won't ever amount to anything in this world.'

'Good lad.'

With my parents, looking for my Invisible Friend, The Milligan

My mother had to be protected from unwholesome influences, like soldiers. Of course she had married one but my father knew when to say, 'Save that sort of talk for the barrack room.' He said it when I was older and when I had a barrack room to go to – but he also said it, for practice I suppose, when I was a boy and my brother had come along and we were experimenting with naughty words like bum.

Once *en famille* we all went to the Garrison Theatre, or Gaff, and saw a variety show. Two comedians were doing their act and one pointed to the other's starched shirt front (known as a dickie) that was curling up and said, 'Your dickie's hanging out.' My father was furious. 'Call that family entertainment?' he snarled. 'Come on. Let's go.'

'No, sit down, Arthur,' said my mother. 'It's nearly over. We don't want to disturb everybody.'

As we walked home over the fields, shining our dimmed torches, Dad said, 'You can't go anywhere these days. After the war's over we'll all be able to stay indoors.'

So basically we stayed home a lot. My brother (Roger) and I had a sheltered childhood. A lot of it in air-raid shelters. Larkhill, Brighton, Exeter in time for the blitz, and back to Larkhill. My father gained promotion to Regimental Sergeant Major, WO I, Instructor of Gunnery. As a teacher, a fine one too with a good mind for mathematics, he was too valuable to send abroad to fight. He could train twenty men every six months to go and do that. He wanted to go abroad and constantly volunteered. Only when the war was over did they send him to India.

India, where he had spent four years before the war. A few weeks before he embarked he had met my mother – heard a woman singing in the next room when he was in a pub – 'Who owns that lovely voice?' he had demanded. It belonged to Trixie, Child of The Light, ever to be protected against unwholesome influences (though she was slightly older than him).

They had had a whirlwind romance. He had proposed and she had accepted – then off he went to the farthest reaches of the Empire. Absence makes the heart grow fonder. He was a handsome man, our Arthur, with his Ronald Coleman moustache. However he suffered a facial stroke while in India. When he came home, after his four years' absence, he said, 'Do you still want me?'. 'It's hardly noticable,' said Trixie, and they were shortly thereafter wed. Thus was the scenario set for my absurd childhood.

My mother often told us boys, 'There's one golden rule in this family. Your father and I never argue in front of the children.'

'That's us,' said Roger. 'Isn't it, Mum?'

'Yes,' she said.

It meant that when Arthur shouted at us, which he often did, she could not take our side. Her Boys. Apart from an occasional, 'Oh, Arthur' and his retort, 'Go on. Take their part. You want them to rule the roost, do you? Let John tell us what time dinner is and if we should turn up to the table with muddy faces. In fact he can fight Hitler and I'll go to bed.'

Little did he know that I spent my days roaming the fields, dreaming of winning the war. I was often a spy on some secret vital mission to Germany. It was all arranged so that I could leave at night – possibly by rocket – and be back in time for school in the morning, with no-one any the wiser. It was only when I was killed in action, as was invariably the conclusion of my day dream, that the truth came out. I did an impression of a trumpet playing the Last Post and imagined my grieving parents at my graveside.

'If only we had known,' said Arthur. 'We'd have understood why he was too tired to do his homework. No wonder he was getting B minuses at school and reports like, he doesn't seem to be with us half the time.'

Dad was often away on a Gunnery Course at Shoeburyness, a welcome respite for The Boys, a chance to lift their heads over the parapet and be naughty. In fact to go wild, whooping over fields, plantations and gunnery ranges.

'I'll tell your father,' Mum used to say – about the latest infringement – but she was hopeless at discipline herself, prone to break out in tears of laughter. Dad was the heavy. To be fair he was set up by her. We all had our roles to play.

My childhood was an emotional cauldron. A soft Mum, a hard Dad, ridiculous views – standing to attention in front of the radio when it played the National Anthem before the King's speech Christmas Day. All quite bonkers.

I was bombed in Exeter in 1943, while Spike was bombed in Italy. Hitler was out to get us both and stop Goon humour.

Adolph and Goebbels.

'Why are the British fools always laughing? We will give them something to laugh at. Bomb Milligan and Antrobus. AND GET ERIC SYKES!'

'Yah, Mein Führer.' By the way we have heard that Private Johnny Speight – another English swine humorist – is working in the cookhouse on the Second Front.'

'Leave him there! He is worth a Panzer Gruppe where he is.'

'Yah, Mein Führer! Time for your enema…'

Spike's childhood in India. Army.

Mine in England. Army.

Both fathers Regimental Sergeant Majors.

My father as a Sergeant would have been in India when RSM Milligan was there. They might have met in the Sergeant's Mess in Delali, Indian School of Gunnery.

RSM Milligan: What will you have to drink, Arthur?

Sgt Antrobus: Whatever you're having.

RSM Milligan: I'm not having anything. That was a cheap round. I heard that you're heading back to Blighty soon, Arthur? Lucky man.

Sgt Antrobus: Yes, I'm expecting to marry a girl called Trixie. I first heard her singing in a public house. She's got a lovely voice.

RSM Milligan: So has my wife. I first heard her shouting at a dog. I thought – in the blink of an eye – one day that woman will be shouting at me.

Sgt Antrobus: How romantic. How is young Terrance?(*not yet called Spike*) Is he growing up?

RSM Milligan: No, he's growing down. But this has the effect of pushing him upwards.

Sgt Antrobus: He is a wonderfully happy lad.

RSM Milligan: I'm teaching him to box.

Sgt Antrobus: That's good. So that he can stand up to the other boys?

RSM Milligan: No, so that he can stand up to his mother. I need some assistance.

Sgt Antrobus: Does she throw crockery at you, Leo?

RSM Milligan: Only if it needs washing up.

Sgt Antrobus: Ah, the bliss of domesticity. Very settling. Before I depart to England I must sadly shoot my dog.

RSM Milligan: You can give him to Terrance.

Sgt Antrobus: Really? If you say so, Leo. But I don't know what a young boy would do with a dead dog.

RSM Milligan: He can bury it.

Sgt Antrobus: What a good idea. What are you having? My round, Leo…

'Before'

'After'

Magical childhoods. Absurd parents who cared, nevertheless, for their offspring and fought to make a better world for them. And Spike, older than me, went to war. We both survived and was it the closeness of the exploding bombs that dislocated our minds? Or were we born to fall apart into fragments and spend the rest of our lives putting the bits together? Was it one jigsaw puzzle or two? Because I think I've got pieces of Spike's sky in my picture. Which would explain the black shapes he sees.

Spike and I were in Fu Tong's, Kensington High Street, one lunch time when Terry Thomas joined us. He came in from the street throwing his hat, coat, gloves and socks at the waiter and exclaimed…

'I've just met an absolute bounder! Taxi cab bloke who asked me for my autograph while the clock was still running!'

The gap in Terry's teeth loomed over us…

'I wrote, "To Bill – a cad of a cabby – the meanest bastard on the ranks!" We'd already been through a car wash and changed a flat tyre in Hyde Park. They think you'll put up with anything these days. Well, I won't. That's why I only tipped him £5.'

He sat down in a heap of Terry Thomas.

'He looked vaguely like a chap I knew in the war,' he continued, blithely. 'An ambulance driver. Whenever I was wounded this chap would come and collect me. It was an arrangement we had. He'd drop what he was doing and come straight up to the front line.'

Spike and I were already laughing.

'How did he know you were wounded?' spluttered Spike.

'There was a hole in my tunic, for God's sake, Spike. It was smouldering. It was obvious I was wounded. I received the Brent Cross.'

'Don't you mean the Victoria Cross?' I asked, giving him the feed line.

'No, I never go that way home,' Terry smiled beautifically and I saw my reflection in his front molars.

Eric Sykes walked in and handed the waiter his camel hair coat. 'Have that valued,' he said, 'and tell me how much I can afford to eat and drink.' He sat down at our table.

'Hello, Spike. You're looking very well for a man who's only got fifty years to live.'

He turned to the Chinese waiter. 'Egg and chips, please.'

'I give you egg flied rice, Mr Sykes. No egg and chips.'

'Worse than Changhi here, isn't it?' exclaimed Eric. 'And we never get our Red Cross parcels. Where are they?'

Spike said, 'I got a parcel last week. It contained a pair of socks and a knitted escape tunnel.'

'Where did it come out?'

'The Burma Railway.'

Spike is restoring the Elfin Oak in Kensington Palace gardens. The sun is shining and I find him happily engrossed in painting a gnome.

'None of the bastards care except me,' said Spike. He is wearing an Australian bush hat (no corks).

'How did you get permission to do this work?' I asked him.

'I pointed out that there wouldn't be a fairy tree to delight the children if it deteriorated much further. I've had to rebuild this gnome before I painted it. Draw it. Memorise it, then scrape it down and rebuild it. The Head of Parks said what do you know about restoring gnomes, Mr Milligan? I told him I'd been doing it all my life. That I'd worked in a gnome factory in Lewisham before the war. And that I was on my way to being an Inspector of Gnomes when war broke out. I told him, you see a gnome in a garden. Did you know it had been inspected and passed? What for? he asked. "You inspect a gnome," I told him, "for malevolence. A harmless gnome is no good to anyone. They have a power to do mischief, not evil, but if they dislike someone they can give him piles."'

I've already got them,' he said.

'Do you sit on radiators?'

'No. Chairs.'

'No chairs. You must be in a bad way. What's your take-home pay?'

He said, 'I can't go home in case the dog bites me and anyway my wife is living with someone else.'

I said, 'Is he four foot three?'

He said, 'Yes.'

I said, 'He's living with my wife as well. It's obvious a gnome has put a spell on you. If I restore the tree, that'll fix it. So he agreed.'

We are both laughing.

Spike made a lovely job of restoring the fairy tree in Kensington Palace Gardens. It took two years. Would the gnomes ever come and restore Spike, I wondered. One good turn deserves another.

Curious kids were hanging around, asking questions.

'Why are you painting that elf's trousers blue, Spike?'

'He asked me to. He asked me to paint his trousers the colour of the sky.'

'He's lucky it wasn't raining,' said a small boy, 'or he'd have grey trousers, wouldn't he?'

The kids giggled.

'Grey and wet,' said a small girl. 'Like my little brother's trousers'.

I was working with Spike in his office a week later, when I noticed a gnome perched up on the picture rail.

'There's a gnome up there,' I said.

'I know,' said Spike, and continued typing our latest epic. I found it rather disconcerting.

'What's it doing up there?'

'Wondering what we're doing down here,' said Spike.

'Don't you find it unusual?'

'No. But then I'm Irish. I've been seeing gnomes for years.'

Spike stopped typing and stared at me, then looked at the greenish creature.

'Whatever it is, I'm glad you can see it as well. The chances of us both being mad at the same time are less.'

'How long's it been up there?' I enquired.

'Since I started working on the Elfin Oak. It comes and goes. Or maybe it's a different one. They all look the same to me. Like people from Ealing.'

'I expect it's come to say thank you from somewhere,' I said. 'On behalf of the rest of them.'

'Gnomes are notoriously shy,' said Spike. He stood up and

found a camera in a box on the floor. Or was it a drawer from an absent chest of drawers?

'Look, take a picture of me and that gnome, will you?' he asked. 'If it doesn't disappear first, which they often do.'

'OK,' I said, and took quite a good shot of him and the elfin visitor. In fact I took three photographs.

'We'll see if they come out,' said Spike. 'The Power Workers have, so anything's possible.' We got on with our writing and when I glanced up the gnome had vanished.

It must have been two or three weeks after that when we were engaged upon another writing session.

'It's not here today,' I said.

'What?'

'The gnome.'

Before Spike could answer there was a polite tap on the door.

'Either bugger off or come in!' shouted Spike.

A police inspector with a constable entered. 'Sorry to intrude, Mr Milligan. But we have heard some disturbing rumours since you have started working on the Elfin Oak in Kensington Palace Gardens, W2. It seems that you were not willing to leave well alone and have disturbed certain powers.'

'You mean the somnolent Park Committee,' retorted Spike.

'No, the underworld which underpins and is behind all manifestations, Mr Milligan,' said the inspector.

'Am I under arrest? Can I pack a small suitcase?' demanded Spike.

'You can pack what you like, sir.'

'Then I'll phone Pickfords.'

'No, you can't bring all your furniture to Scotland Yard, sir.' The inspector looked appalled.

'Well, who's going to look after it? If I'm not here.'

'But we're not arresting you so it doesn't crop up.'

'Right. What do you want?'

The inspector frowned at me. 'Who is this gentleman?'

'He recently left Sandhurst,' explained Spike.

'Was he posted?'

'No, he was left on the doorstep.'

The inspector took a deep breath, then remembered to breathe out again. 'Right…' He produced a notebook.

'Where did you start seeing gnomes, Mr Milligan?'

'In India,' said Spike. 'They came out in the hot weather.'

'How were they dressed?'

'From head to foot and sometimes backwards.'

The inspector wrote it all down laboriously. 'I see. When did you stop seeing them?'

'When I stopped believing in them.'

The inspector pulled the rubber band back over his notebook, flicked the button on his biro and stood up.

'I should warn you, sir, that these gnomes are not Irish gnomes – or any native variety – but Albanian gnomes. They've been coming into the country in large numbers. The customs officials can do nothing because they don't come through Heathrow. Or Dover. They just materialise where they like. We can't turn them back. I can't have customs officials posted everywhere outguessing them, can I?'

'I'm not going to have one in my office,' said Spike. 'I'd have to show him my passport every time I opened a window.'

'Exactly. We don't wish to intrude upon your work and the valuable contribution to the nation that your humour brings in this time of peril. Gnome-like peril. All I ask, Spike…' the inspector continued, becoming more familiar, 'is that if this gnome appears again you will shake some salt over it – whereupon it will turn into a puddle of water. Soak it up with this piece of blotting paper provided and post it to Scotland Yard in this prepaid envelope.'

The constable produced a salt cellar, a piece of blotting paper and a second-class addressed envelope.

'Anything else?' asked Spike.

'Yes, if you could just sign my autograph book, I'd be most grateful.'

Spike wrote, 'Please return this inspector to Paddington Green police station and collect your deposit, love Light and Peace, Spike Milligran.'

A few days later I visited Spike again, quite eager for news.

'Come in, John,' said Spike, affably, producing a batch of photographs.

'These came back from the chemist's. The ones you took of me and the gnome.'

I peered at the three snapshots I had taken. Spike was there but the picture rail was empty. No sign of a gnome.

'They don't photograph,' said Spike.'I suspected as much.'

'And now we've frightened it, or them, away,' I sighed.

'No,' said Spike. He open a drawer and pulled out a piece of stained blotting paper. 'I've got it here,' he said.

'Are you going to post it to Scotland Yard?'

'Not likely,' said Spike. 'I've posted another piece of blotting paper to the Plods. With a coffee stain. Let them work it out.' He wound a piece of white paper on to the typewriter roller.

'Got any ideas for a Goon Show, John?'

'Bit early for that.'

'Yes, go and get some doughnuts, will you? There's some money on the floor…'

There was money all over the floor.

Fu Tong's again. It seemed that life was a series of hilarious lunches. Harry Secombe comes in blowing a large raspberry.

'It's all in the mind, folks! I've just been to the doctor about this terrible wind! He issued a Force Nine gale warning to all shipping and prescribed three tins of baked beans daily, take one every half mile. So at least I'm getting the exercise…'

He blew another raspberry and sat down at the table, full of giggles. Spike looked indignant.

'You'll get us thrown out of this restaurant, you mad fool!'

'I've just been thrown into it, Spike. A strange coincidence, wouldn't you say?'

Harry blew another raspberry. Spike crossed his eyes.

'I will inform the management it's dangerous to feed you.'

'That's alright. I brought a sandwich. Do you know what's inside it?

Spike: Yes, everything that's not outside it. Including me.

Harry: Correct!

Spike: You force me, sir, to eat elsewhere.

Harry: I thought this was elsewhere. A moment ago I said I'm going elsewhere and I came here.

Spike: As soon as you go somewhere else, it stops being elsewhere.

Harry: That's terrifying. You mean… as soon as I get there, it's here?

Spike: Exactly. The only way to keep somewhere else where it is is never to go there.

Harry: How fascinating! So it's all here then? The whole damn thing?

Spike: It was here all the time.

Harry: My God! You're right… (*Shouts*) Waiter! Waiter, damn you! Set fire to your trousers and produce a menu immediately!'

The waiter approaches with a menu, smiling, in the game.

Waiter: Yes, sir. Coming, Mr Secombe.

Harry: I haven't got time to eat today. I'll just have a bill, please.

Waiter: How big you like it, Mr Secombe, sir?

Harry: What do you suggest?

Waiter: Twenty seven pounds velly good today.

Harry: Splendid. That's sounds right to me. I'll have that. And while I'm waiting I'll have lunch.

Peter Sellers comes in.

Peter (*As Saunders of The River*): Hello. Sorry I'm late… No, I'm not sorry. I'm glad, do you hear me? I'm glad all over. Very very glad it's taken me so long to get here. Yes… You see I bought a new car this morning.

Spike: Did the old one fall off the number plate?

Peter: Yes, you're right, it wasn't securely fastened. I was parking my number plate last night and I noticed that the car had vanished. That and Ying Pong Tiddle I Po.

Spike: With nerdles, I trust?

Peter: Exactly, Spike. With nerdles. It played havoc with my suspension.

Spike: I didn't know you'd been suspended.

Peter: Yes, ever since that business with a guardsman.

Harry: Really? They're not available in my district yet.

Peter: Then you'll have to move if you want that sort of thing, won't you?

Harry: Agreed.

Spike: You filthy swine!

Harry: I didn't know you cared.

Peter: And what are you doing these days, young Johnny?

Me (*Taking notes*): I'm listening.

Spike: He's a listener! Don't let him get away.

Peter: We must get him to a radio set immediately!

Harry: I knew a man who could listen to the radio and view television at the same time in his bath while playing the mandolin and eating porridge through a straw.

Spike: Was he versatile?

Harry: No, Jewish.

Peter: Some of my best mothers are Jewish.

Harry: In that case, take that… (*He blows another raspberry.*)

Peter (*Blows a raspberry*): God, it's catching! (*As Major Bloodnok.*)

The screens, nurse, quickly!

Spike: Waiter! Bring us a new conversation. Number 34.

Me (*As Chinese waiter*): No conversation 34 left, sir. Terry Thomas was in earlier. You can have conversation 22 B with noodles.

Spike: Bring that with the dictionary.

Me: No bring dictionary to table, sir.

Peter: I've just visited the dictionary outside. It's engaged.

Spike: How distressing. You must have been lost for words.

Peter: I was, yes. How did you guess?

Spike: By a study of your urine sample.

Peter: So it came through the post?

Spike: No, it came through the roof.

Peter: I've never been on your roof, sir. Needle, nardle, noo to you!

Spike: You can say that again.

Peter: I didn't even say it the first time. It's a record I'm playing.

Spike: And here's a photograph of me eating lunch with you.

Harry: And here's a green blancmange statuette of John Antrobus paying the bill. An astonishing likeness, isn't it?

Peter: So it is, by George. I'll eat it later. It reminds me of the time we were in Fu Tong's together. Good times, weren't they? You can never bring them back, you know.

That was the last time I had lunch with the Goons. It was one long lunch but one day it was over. Like you don't know it's the last day... until you look back and say, 'It's history. I was there.' But it didn't feel like history. It was just lunch at Fu Tong's as usual. You had the money. You didn't think about spending it. There would always be more. There would always be more money. And other days. And crazy company. But that was the last day I can remember that we sat together and had number 22 B conversation with noodles.

Another day. I am waiting for Spike in his office. On impulse I open a drawer and take out the piece of stained blotting paper. Spike walks in.

'What are you doing?'

'Looking at the gnome. What's left of it. How do we get it back?'

'We'll go to Scotland Yard and ask that Inspector. Come on.'

We caught a taxi and went to the large building near St James's Park tube station that housed the hub of police thinking. You could hear it throbbing.

'Wait here,' said Spike to the taxi driver and we entered reception.

By some miracle of police organisation we found ourselves in the inspector's office. He was packing away his few belongings and the room looked empty, ransacked – the same as his face.

'Hello, Spike,' he said. 'I'm taking early retirement. I'm only in the force for another five minutes. What do you want?'

'I've come about the gnome...'

'Forget that,' said the retiring policeman. He shut the office door and faced us with a haunted look.

'Forget all about Albanian gnomes. Officially they don't exist. They won't be in the statistics of gnomes this year. Not that I care. I'll be in Torremolinos with Gilbert Harding…'

While the inspector rambled on, Spike beckoned me towards the wastepaper basket. It was full of pieces of stained blotting paper. I stuffed them into my pockets.

'Look,' said Spike, 'how do we release the gnomes? As they don't officially exist you can tell me… HOW WOULD YOU LIKE TO BE STUCK IN A PIECE OF BLOTTING PAPER FOR THE REST OF YOUR LIFE?' shouted Spike, who could play the heavy.

The inspector looked shocked.

'Bake the blotting paper over a woodsmoke fire,' he muttered.

'Any magic words?'

'Yes. Don't forget to bung a copper.'

Spike bunged him £50 and we left.

Spike directed the taxi to take us to Highgate, to the fringes of a small wood. Midst the trees stood an ominous-looking sanitised white building. Even though the sun was strong, there were no shadows to be seen.

'That's my old nuthouse,' said Spike. 'The puzzle factory. I once spent three months in there.'

We ventured into the wood and built a fire of twigs and dead branches and soon it was crackling away. I found a piece of corrugated tin. We laid it over the fire, propping it up on bricks and put the pieces of blotting paper on it.

'Get some green wood, John.'

I did as I was bidden and chucked the wood on to the flames. A dense smoke swirled around us. We could hear the blotting paper sizzling.

'I hope this works,' said Spike.

A gnome plopped out of the smoke. On its boots was written, 'Made in Albania'. Plunging off the tin, through the smoke round about us, one gnome after another appeared.

'Count them!' shouted Spike.

'Why?'

'It will help you sleep!'

When the smoke cleared the gnomes had vanished.

'Why did we do that?' I asked Spike.

'Albanian gnomes can't be more stupid than Irish gnomes,' he replied. 'And they don't do Irish clog dances on my picture rail.'

A man appeared, strolling out of the trees, pipe in one hand, a walking stick in the other and a bottle opener dangling from his belt.

'Oh, hello, Spike,' he said. 'Are you feeling any better?'

'Yes, thank you, Doctor Robson.'

'We'd better be getting back inside,' said the now named medical person. 'It's going to rain. What were you doing with that fire?'

'Releasing Albanian gnomes,' said Spike. 'They were being persecuted.'

'Oh, I see,' said Doctor Robson. We'll have to change your medication. Just drop your trousers and cough, will you?'

But we were running through the woods, back to the taxi and home to the office. Back to work. Some days you don't feel like writing. But you start... putting words down... anything, as it comes... and if you're lucky you might get a gnome story.

Suddenly I knew. I knew what I had forgotten about the recording of the second Goon Show I had co-written with Spike. It was a row between him and Peter Sellers that had blown up out of a blue sky... Spike loved books. He read them, bought them, collected them, indeed he had a library. He loved books.

Whenever Spike lent a book to me (or anyone else) he would stick a yellow memo inside the back cover, 'Please return to Spike Milligan.' He anguished if a book went missing yet when he spoke with passion about a book to a friend he would often lend it out. Thus the agony began...

'You've got my *Battle of El Alamein* haven't you, John?'

'Yes, Spike. I'm reading it.'

'OK. No hurry to return it.'

A few days later a phone call. Midnight.

'John, is it right you've got my book? *The Battle of El Alamein*?'

'Yes, Spike, I've nearly finished it. Do you want me to bring it over now?'

'No. No hurry. I wanted to be sure where it was.'

'Well, put a pin in your map of missing books in Pimlico.'

Spike, laughing, 'Goodnight, John!'

'Goodnight, Spike!'

A week later. A telegram arrives at my home:

'I cannot find Bertrand Russell's *A History of Western Philosophy*. Have you got it? Love. Spike.'

I get on the phone. 'I haven't got Bertrand Russell's. But I'm on page 243 of *The Battle of El Alamein*, if you'd like to make a note of it.'

'Oh, good. That's one I don't need to worry about.'

'I'll bring it in on Monday, Spike.'

'OK.'

I always returned Spike's books. Even if he lost track of what I had. I'm like that. He got *El Alamein* back and I don't know about *A History of Western Philosophy* but he never mentioned it to me again.

It was *The Battle For Spien Kop* that did it.

At rehearsal, one Goon show Sunday, Spike was distracted, fluffing his lines. Peter Sellers looked concerned.

Peter: What's upsetting you, Spike?

Spike: I've lost *The Battle For Spien Kop*, that's what's upsetting me.'

Peter (*laughing*): That was lost years ago!

Spike: My book, you fool. You wouldn't have borrowed it because you're semi-illiterate. Like the company you keep. Your famous friends.

Peter: Princess Margaret reads a lot.

Spike: She doesn't need to read. It's like doing her own laundry and cleaning her own shoes. She can get a servant to read her books.

Peter (*no longer laughing*): Oh, yes? Well you're jealous of my friends because you can't keep any. I hope you never find that book *The Battle For Spien Kop*. And I hope you lose a lot more books, Spike. I hope you lose a library full of books.

Spike: And I hope you lose your wife, your money, your health and your mind.

Peter: Then I'd be like you, wouldn't I, Spike? Except that you'd always be worse off than me. Because you've also lost *The Battle For Spien Kop*.

They didn't speak to each other for weeks. But the Goon Show recordings did not suffer. They were too professional for that.

Eventually Peter gave Spike a present. A copy of *The Battle For Spien Kop*.

'Thank you,' said Spike. 'Now I've got two copies of that one. All I need is *A History of Western Philosophy* and I'll be very happy.

So Peter bought him that as well.

Spike said, 'I'd still like to know the bastard who can't be bothered to return my books.'

The original copy of *The Battle For Spien Kop* had been returned to Milligan anonymously. The plain package that had arrived through the post bore a W.1 postmark, so The Milligan had searched through his address book to see who lived there.

I pointed out, 'Look, Spike, nobody would be that stupid, would they? And post it from the district where they live. They'd get a taxi to another area and post it there. So they could still visit you and be friendly and borrow more books. And destroy your peace of mind and drive you back to the nut-house.'

'I'll get the bastard one day,' said Spike.

I sold a story to Peter Rogers, the producer of all the Carry On films. It was called *The Big Job*. I wrote the first screenplay. The job went round the office. Next Peter Rogers commissioned Galton and Simpson to write a further screenplay. Then it came to be Spike's turn. At this stage it was called *The Great Spinoza*. He wrote the script out in beautiful copperplate pen, so much did he love the script. It was as if a medieval monk had produced the text. I did not read it but it looked beautiful.

If you were lucky enough to get an autograph from Spike or a dedication, he always took his time and wrote it out with great care, loops and twirls. He loved the very act of writing and would not be hurried. What he was doing became the most important thing in the world. Either that or he would not do it at all.

Too ill.

I was still determined to succeed as a playwright. I was entranced by theatre and particularly the Royal Court with its offerings from John Osborne, Arnold Wesker, Ionesco, N F Simpson and Anne Jellico, though she told me in later days she did not care for my play *Trixie And Baba*, I did not revise my high opinion of *The Sport Of My Mad Mother*. Then there was the outstanding Sunday Night production by Lindsey Anderson of *The Lily White Boys* by Christopher Logue.

Across the other side of town was Joan Littlewood. *A Taste Of Honey* at the Theatre Royal Stratford. I saw Brendan Behan's *The Hostage* at the Watergate theatre club and *Cat On a Hot Tin Roof*. All these authors and their plays astonished me and I longed to join their ranks. I wanted to be an Angry Young Man, but I was far too good natured, still writing comedy for the likes of Morecambe and Wise. However out of this dichotomy would spring a work written in association with Spike Milligan – a fruitful act of co-authorship – in which our mutual talents peaked to please the world and line our pockets with yet more lolly. Despite bouts of heavy drinking I was able to bring the best of myself to this work and its production. It would become a triumph critically. SOLD OUT. HOUSE FULL. I had made it, with my friend Spike.

But from the glittering heights, as I surveyed a wondrous future, I was to fall like a stone into obscurity, alcoholism, debt and visits to a mental hospital. It was me I would be visiting...

It's easier to look back than to look forward, isn't it?

The play was called *The Bedsitting Room*.

Around that time, I met with George Devine, who was Artistic Director at the Royal Court, responsible for the English Stage Company there and its great output. He took me to a lunch in a grey-washed wall restaurant off the King's Road and brought his new assistant along, a chap called Bill Gaskill who sat on the edge of his chair, it being his first day, but never looked back after that.

I had earlier sent a few pages to George, in long hand of course, about this idea... A man who fears he will turn into a bedsitting room, which he does, and the dubious doctor he has been seeing moves in with his fiancée, declaring that it will be easier to work a cure on the premises. Therein lies the dilemna. For the doctor to heal the condition would mean him becoming homeless.

The Royal Court were interested. Some time later I met with Bernard Miles from the Mermaid and he commissioned a play from me, unspecified as to title and subject.

I had also told Spike the outline story of this would be play, and he – much entertained – told his own version of it at various dinner parties, adding the fact that it all took place after a nuclear attack when the poor man, Lord Fortnum of Alamein, had mutated into a bedsitting room, despite having his own personal early warning radar system in his top hat that gave him that extra four minutes in bed.

Then along came a group called Tomorrow's Audience, which included Willy Rushton and Richard Ingrams – among its unknown players. Also aboard was Peter Rawley, later to become Milligan's agent for a limited season.

They contacted Spike and asked him if he had a one-act play they could perform.

Spike came back to me and said, 'What are you doing with that idea called *The Bedsitting Room*, John?' and I said, 'Well...' and he said, 'How about we write it up together for these lads?'

'OK.'

I went to his office and the job was soon done.

Came the production at the Marlowe Theatre, Canterbury. Tomorrow's Audience invited Kenneth Tynan, the top critic on Sunday's *Observer* to attend and he let all concerned know he was coming.

When Spike heard the news he was mightily unpleased and forthwith sent The Great And Noble Critic a telegram (Spike sent lots of telegrams), begging him not to come to Canterbury as *The Bedsitting Room* was work in progress. Being myself an author in progress, I was not concerned.

The First Night audience loved the play and Spike and I took a bow, gratified it had gone so well. While bowing Spike caught sight of The Esteemed Observer Critic sitting in the audience taking notes, and nearly fell into the orchestra pit.

Kenneth Tynan devoted his full column the next Sunday to praising the play. We were already a hit.

Monday morning about 7.30 a.m. I received a phone call from Bernard Miles. This was the play he had commissioned. He had the contract to prove it. 'Hello, John. About *The Bedsitting Room*. How soon can you and Spike write it up into a full evening's entertainment for the Mermaid? 'Cos I've booked you in for next February.'

So the Royal Court went out of the window. I suppose because they got up later than Bernard Miles on Monday morning.

At that time Spike was appearing at the Mermaid Theatre for B. Miles, playing Ben Gunn in *Treasure Island*. I went along and wrote the new scenes for our play with this Ben Gunn creature, when he was not onstage, and sometimes when he was. I remember writing with a toothless, straggly bearded, long-haired castaway clothed in rags and a cosmetic tanning product, who longed for cheese.

Ben Gunn: Cheese! Cheese! A blue-veined Stilton smelling of socks!

Me: Not until we have written this scene, Ben.

Ben Gunn: What is that instrument?

Me: A typewriter.

Ben Gunn: Does it make cheese? A crumbling Cheshire. A loamy Leicester. A gorgeous Gorgonzola…

Me: No, Ben, no…

Ben Gunn: Then what use is it to me? I want a stinking ripe French Camembert that wafts a thousand miles sending chattering monkeys wild. Stampeding herds of pigs and sending poor Ben Gunn salivating, scampering on the beach his nostrils extended towards the East, sniffing! Ah, CHEESE!

Me: With this typewriter, Mr Gunn, we can write ourselves off Treasure Island. Escape the pirates! Up, up and away…

Ben Gunn: Into a cheese shop! Good. Let's do it. Continue…

Ben blinks and scratches his chest to find a flea and taste it, as I write.

Ben Gunn (*craftily*): What is this piece we are composing, Mr Antrobus? Would you say?

Me: It is a piece for theatre, Mr Gunn. And you will play Spike Milligan playing Mate, a traffic warden of no fixed parking meter.

Ben Gunn: This Spike Milligan I am to play? This fellow? Does he adore cheese, by any chance?

Me: Moderately so.

Ben Gunn: Moderately so? There is nothing moderate about a liking for cheese! What nonsense. I'll stay Ben – Ben Gunn – and take my chance on Treasure Island. I've yet to milk a monkey and perhaps make monkey cheese…

Who was I with? Who sat beside me raving? Spike Milligan? Ben Gunn? Or Mate, the traffic warden? What's in a name?

'A cheese by any other name will smell as strong.'

Three characters in search of an author. I was haunted by Pirandello. The upshot was the play was writ, by whom I know not, excepting that I was there and who can nail down reality? Each hammer blow becomes memory subject to distortion. So where were we?

We were in the dressing room overlooking the Thames. That was before they built a motorway along the foreshore. Spike had the room done out like a grotto – a cave of delights – and when children came backstage to meet him, he gave them chocolate gold sovereigns and was Ben Gunn again for them, but let's not go into that.

The completed manuscript was delivered to the Mermaid.

Spike left for Australia and things went quiet. It had already been decided that he and I would direct the show but I was more than surprised when Bernard Miles phoned me up one Friday evening and said he required the set designs by the following Monday morning.

'Spike's in Australia,' he said. 'So it's down to you, John.'

Bernard Miles spoke with the plainness of a farmer comparing turnips but he had a peasant's guile. He knew how to get more for his money.

Spike's unbounded faith in our diverse talents left me little option. I went to bed over the weekend where (like the famous authoress) I often did my best work. Although I had not designed so much as a paper clip before, I cheerfully imagined the stage and what we might put upon it. The Mermaid boasts a wonderful acting

Sketch designs for the set
by John Antrobus

area and I had the good sense not to clutter it. After all this was a post-nuclear world. What was left? An immense pile of boots, centre stage, army war surplus, upon which perched on a ladder we would find Captain Martin Bules, VC and pin, pairing boots in the opening scene. As to a shop window, or a door, whoever required such artefacts… bring on your own front door and ring the bell, was the order of the day.

There was a skeleton tree with a mechanical bird that when prodded with a giant finger on a stick, warbled. And two reversible screens set on either side of the stage with political slogans like, 'Labour Loves London' and 'Only The Tories Care.' As there were only thirteen inhabitants left in England, there were not that many to care about. They each took it in turn to be the Monarch, and our play opened with the tune of the National Anthem and the cast singing, 'God save Mrs Gladys Scrokes of Number Seven Blenheim Crescent…'

VALENTINE DYALL
(Wearing his four-minute early warning hat)

Born in the pleasant peasant village of Black, his happiest childhood memories were of frightening the other children. So much so that all his playmates went to Seed, a neighbouring borough. Became known as the Child in Black, and within two hundred years grew to be the Man in Black.

(From programme, Duke of York's Theatre)

The audience rose, as was the custom in those days (though with ever more reluctance) for 'The Queen' and then sat down again in disarray and giggles. I never saw anyone upset, not even Princess Margaret when she came to see the play. Having a tune played repeatedly for your sister must have been pretty boring.

We rehearsed in the January of 1962 which was cold and snowy. Graham Stark was Captain Martin Bules; Valentine Dyall

SPIKE MILLIGAN

This heavily posed portrait is of Spike
Milligan (seen here at the close of
World War II). He was born in India
at the close of World War I. He now
appears at the close of World War III
in the play you are about to see.
Decorated several times for gallantry
for emptying Arab dustbins in the heat
of the battle, Mr. Milligan is now at
work on the statue of World War IV,
portions of which will be available in
the interval.

JOHN ANTROBUS
(Co-author)

While John's parents were on holiday
in the South of France he was born
in Woolwich Hospital. Having learned
to write he dropped them a line, and
they collected him from the out-
patients' department and took him
home to celebrate his twenty-first birthday. He left the next morning for the
Military Academy at Sandhurst to
finish his education. It was here he
was schooled in lunacy, which he has
since taken up as a profession.

(From programme, Duke of York's Theatre.
Both of us looking impossibly beautiful!)

The Bedsi

By John Antr

THE CAST

Captain Bules Martin	GRAHAM STARK
Lord Fortnum of Alamein	VALENTINE DYALL
Mate	SPIKE MILLIGAN
Shelter Man	JOHN BLUTHAL
Plastic mac man	JOHN BLUTHAL
Underwater Vicar	JOHN BLUTHAL
Lord Hume	JOHN BLUTHAL
Cupboard	MARJIE LAWRENCE
Penelope	MARJIE LAWRENCE
Diplomat	BOB TODD
1st Announcer	BOB TODD

(This is the centre-page of the programme from The Mermaid Theatre, original production)

There will be on

Directed

JOHN ANTROBU

ting Room.

s or Spike Milligan

THE CAST

Sea Captain	BOB TODD
2nd Announcer	JOHNNY VYVYAN
Driver	JOHNNY VYVYAN
Chinaman	JOHNNY VYVYAN
Seaman	JOHNNY VYVYAN
Coffin man	CLIVE ELLIOTT

and THE TEMPERANCE SEVEN

Act 1   Captain Bules Martin's
surgery and Government
surplus store

Act 2   Scene 1 Lord Fortnum,
the room.
Scene 2 Lord Fortnum, the
well known room.

terval of 15 minutes

designed by
d SPIKE MILLIGAN

with his deep basement bargain voice (radio's *Man In Black*) played Lord Fortnum of Alamein who was suffering from the fear of mutating into a bedsitting room and hoped it wouldn't happen in Paddington, which of course it did. Bad news.

Bules, and his well known fiancée, Penelope (played by Marjorie Lawrence) moved in and set up house. Later they had their first monster, poignantly shown by three baby socks on a line of washing.

Spike played Mate, the roving traffic warden, who carried a parking meter with him and banged it down in front of anyone, declaring, 'You can't park 'ere, sir.' He had a packet of Daz slung across his chest, over his post-nuclear rags, but what had survived the devastation was the petty tyrant with the crap job.

Mate assailed a bemused Lord Fortnum (before his transformation) and pointed out that he was wearing a packet of Tide in a Daz area. Spike, to make the point, burst into song:

> Whatever you 'as!
> You got to have Daz…
> You get all the dirt
> Off the front of your shirt
> With Daz, Daz, Daz!

The Lord Chamberlain's office was issuing licences to perform in theatre and each play text (unless done in a private club theatre, like the Watergate) would be censored by them. One of their fatuous instructions was…

Omit: 'You get all the dirt, Off the back of your shirt.

Substitute: 'You get all the dirt, Off the front of your shirt.'

What labyrinthine fears lurked in their minds, these Our Masters who knew better, custodians of Public Virtue? Why was 'dirt on the back of your shirt' corrupting, and 'dirt on the front of your shirt' alright?

How long had they discussed this? More understanding was the standard, Omit 'fucking'.

Did the typist blush who made out the licence? Or was it all in the day's work?

Omit: 'fuck off'.

Substitute: 'bugger off'.

This hilarious piece of literature was read out on the satire programme, *That Was The Week That Was* and it all helped towards the collapse of the house of cards of censorship in the theatre.

Official, that is. Now we are all busy censoring ourselves and wondering whether we are P.C .

Spike as Mate was in charge of a couple of men who were carrying an atom bomb between them. Our means of delivery in straitened times had been the postal service, but our bomb had been returned 'insufficient stamps'. Nobody was sure who had won the war, but they knew Britain had lost.

Marjorie Lawrence also played the part of the Chest Of Drawers. She had mutated into a dejected and mottled piece of furniture with a flecked mirror and complained that a Pakistani seaman was taking advantage of her, keeping his curry powders in her drawers.

John Bluthal played various parts with elan, including the Rubber Man, in which part he enters dressed in shreds of black plastic, crying out…

'Beware the perils of the rubber! Rubber! Rubber! Rubber! Stretch and repent!'

Then leads the cast in the song:

You dirty young devil how dare you presume
To piss in the bed when the po's in the room.
I'll wallop your bum with a dirty big broom
When I get up in the morning time!'

The Lord Chamberlain's office left this lyric alone, probably considering it was an Ancient Celtic verse of mystical origins.

Also in the cast were Bob Todd and Johnny Vivian, adding comic texture to the proceedings. The music was played by The Temperance Seven who sat in majesty in a giant picture frame upstage.

The part of the Prime Minister, Harold Macmillan, who had mutated into a parrot, was cast only after auditions. These were well attended not only by six parrots but also by the Press and TV. The publicity stunt suggested by my wife, Maggie, worked a treat.

I solemnly addressed each bird with the question,

'What would be your interpretation of playing the part of Prime Minister?'

One of them, an interesting looking macaw, answered me with a squawk and a bird dropping.

I said, 'I see you've tabled a motion, sir,' and gave him the role.

The bird was a tempestuous performer, prone to nipping passers-by, a drama queen if ever there was one and the only living thing on the set that could upstage Spike Milligan.

This macaw lodged with Bernard Miles and I believe there was a show business link which helped it to get the part.

After the first few days of rehearsal Spiked handed over the entire direction of the play to me so that he could concentrate on the part of Mate. Wisely, I did not question whether I was up to it but continued with the job in hand.

Spike then became nervous as to his capabilities in the role of Mate but Graham Stark assured him he would do well and encouraged him to stay the course. Spike soldiered on.

I told him, 'You can act, don't worry.'

Spike oscillated between believing this, and wanting to destroy everything around him and say 'I told you so. It's rubbish.'

Sticking him to the part was sometimes difficult but if he was not grounded in it, the play would not be served. To improvise, to invent, was not always the best thing. Eventually he knuckled down and learnt his lines (and seemed surprised to find them funny) and we all breathed a sigh of relief.

The previews came and went. And the audiences were purring. I gave some comps to our cleaning lady. She laughed like a drain all the way through then said to me afterwards, 'I don't know what that was all about!'

The First Night was a star-studded affair and a BBC TV news team was in the foyer recording the arrivals, among them Peter Sellers and Harry Secombe. The house was brimful, seated in anticipation and the critics had sharpened pencils at the ready. The question was… would Spike's nerves hold? Because if he started improvising and lost the play, we might as well not have bothered. He had a sound vessel that would support him if he trusted it. The lights went down. The audience arose as The Temperance Seven produced a drum roll for the National Anthem. The cast led the way with, 'God bless Mrs Gladys Scrokes of number seven Blenheim Crescent! Long live Mrs Gladys Scrokes of number seven Blenheim Crescent…'

The audience collapsed with laugher and we never looked back. Spike played his part – the tyrannical upstart traffic warden – with controlled sincerity and was a hit. In one scene Captain Martin Bules and Penelope who are unsuccessfully trying to have a child, adopt Mate. Spike wanders in sucking on a baby's bottle. They say 'coee, coee' and Spike says, 'Piss off.'

'Darling, his first words, "piss off",' says Captain Bules.

The notices were uniformly ecstatic. Goon humour had transferred to the stage and the extended run at the Mermaid had people queueing for returns every night. The play transferred to the Duke of York's theatre in St Martin's Lane. The Temperance Seven were dropped for budgetary reasons and Alan Claire who worked out seven times cheaper was hired to provide the music.

Gone also was Graham Stark who had been a brilliantly funny Captain Martin Bules but who had not got along with Spike, and vice versa. His leaving the play was dramatic. Towards the end of the run at the Mermaid Spike phoned his home and spoke to Audrey Stark who was eight months pregnant.

He said, 'Tell your husband that if he comes to the theatre tonight I will shoot him.'

Graham and Audrey were inclined to put it down to an extravagance on Spike's behalf when the bell rang and Patricia Milligan, Spike's then wife, fell through the door in tears. (The Milligans lived not far away on Hadleigh Common.) She begged Graham not to go the theatre that night, saying she was convinced Spike had a gun and meant what he said.

Then the Mermaid management stepped in and banned Graham from entering the theatre for his own safety. The understudy went on until the transfer.

News at the time was patchy. Even I, as director, did not know half the story. That Graham Stark was unfairly treated is indisputable. For the good of the production, 100% professional that he is, Graham did not leak the story nor take action against anyone. Thank you, Graham.

That Spike could on occasions behave monstrously most people know. What had triggered this behaviour? A psychological trauma surfacing? Did he imagine it was all good clean fun? A prank? Or perhaps artistic licence? Genius making it's own laws…

What might not have helped…

When both George C. Scott and Stanley Kubrick (separately) came to the theatre, they loved the play and had gone back stage, but only to visit Graham Stark (who anyway knew Kubrick).

'Aren't you going to pop in and say hello to Spike?' suggested Graham to Kubrick.

'No, you can't be sure how you'll find him,' said Kubrick. And they went off to supper. The same thing happened with George C. Scott and his wife. No visit to Milligan's dressing room from the Hollywood top table.

Spike did not like to be overlooked.

He already felt overshadowed by the burgeoning inter-national film career of Peter Sellers. There was a sibling rivalry between them even when they were the best of friends. *The Bedsitting Room* had opened up new vistas for Spike. He only had to hang in there. To clock in and do the work.

But he would sometimes take against the audience when things did not go his way, let them know of his displeasure if they did not react well to his ad-libs. (Remember Coventry!) An audience could be the amorphous THEM. Perhaps Spike felt threatened by THEM some nights. They outnumbered him. He wanted the golden moments of their adulation and applause. He did not like to admit he was hooked on the drug of their approval. So to prove he wasn't Spike would scorn them some nights.

'There you see! I don't care what you think of me…'

Some hidden agenda would intrude and spoil the simple pleasures he could bestow with the unique talents he undoubtedly possessed and instead we would get a spiteful (rather than Spikeful) performance.

So Stanley Kubrick and George C. Scott did not knock upon his dressing-room door – so what? We all feel neglected from time to time without necessarily getting into a rage.

Over to Anthony Clare…

He had Spike in his TV show, called *In The Psychiatrist's Chair*, and asked him:

'What do you consider to be your most glaring defect?'

Spike pondered awhile.

'I haven't got one.'

Did he have a gun? Spike himself told me that a police sergeant had called round to make enquiries, coming to his dressing room and asked him straight did he have a gun? Spike produced a children's toy cap pistol.

'Bang, bang, sergeant.'

'Who's to know that's not real, Mr Milligan?'

'Ooch, yerp.' As Eccles.

'You must promise never to do that again.'

'I promise. Scout's honour. Anyone for wine?'

When the police visitors had gone Spike took a real gun from under his couch and decided to take it home that night.

Barry Humphries came in to play Captain Martin Bules at the Duke of Yorks, and he got along with Spike well enough. Barry was very funny, making the part his own. Perhaps his own brand of bizarre humour made him more amenable to Milligan.

One night, Spike was off ill. But he phoned from his Highgate home to ask to speak to Humphries.

'He's on stage,' said the stage doorman.

'I know exactly when he's onstage,' said Spike. 'Put me through.'

The stage doorman hung up.

Spike summoned a taxi to the West End, told the driver to wait, and limping with a walking stick went to the theatre's stage door. He aimed a blow at the doorman (who was on danger money), 'Don't tell me when Barry Humphries is onstage!' shouted Spike, who did not enjoy being contradicted, and returned to his taxi, thence homeward to Highgate.

Yes, Spike was a man of strange moods. Better not to hang up on him. I wonder did he see himself as an epic figure who had to leave some stories of himself for posterity?

Those were two examples.

What drove you on, Spike Milligan? You were not always led by angels. You were sometimes driven by demons.

Never mind Spike's problems. I had some of my own…

We are in Dublin. A couple of years later. *The Bedsitting Room* is on tour after another production in the West End. The money had kept rolling in, enough to keep me in booze – none put by – and fame only fanned the flames of my Bonfire of Vanities. I was still trying to fix myself with money, applause, sex and rock and roll. God, I tried. I didn't give up easily. I was intent on creating a myth of myself as the alcoholic artist. I still had some catching up to do on Brendan Behan…

Meanwhile I had found Spike on tour. He was kindness itself to me, though I was stubble-bearded, haunted, dissolute, he took me out to dinner. He was stubble-bearded too, come to think of it, but there the resemblance ended. He probably lent me £50, an advance from the box office, though he wouldn't care if he got it back or not.

I was on the run from my marriage. I could not simply make the break but neither could I stay. So I kept coming and going like a shuttlecock. Spike listened to my woes. My troubles. I could still hear the crockery smashing… which had nothing to do with drink, of course. He did not offer advice, he offered friendship. He was there for me and simply told me I would find my own way through.

As has been remarked, I had a basic problem in that my behaviour was deteriorating more quickly than I could lower my standards.

Spike had been asked to do a TV interview, a chat show where he would advertise our play being in Dublin that week. Having nothing better to do, I went along with him to the studios.

The interviewer was pleasantness itself.

'Well, Spike, I expect you'll be doing your own zany, goony thing, won't you, so I've told the camera crew to follow you round the studio. Whatever you get up to, they'll be there recording you and your antics, right?'

Spike sat slumped in his chair. He had taken a dislike to the man.

'Just ask the questions,' he muttered.

'Right. Just so long as you know that if you feel like getting up and wandering around, that's FINE by us. This will not be a formal interview with a lot of stupid questions, if you get my meaning? I'm not going to fence you in…'

Spike kept silent. The warning signals were going out.

'You have a rare reputation, Spikey, for improvising – throwing the rule book out of the window! So we're just going to give you your head. This is FUN TIME! It's all up to you, Spike Milligan. So off we go then…'

They started recording. The first thirty seconds were fine as the interviewer introduced Spike. Then, as he had no prepared questions, he sat back beaming and waited for The Milligan's response. The Black Hole of depression opposite him drew in the studio light, withering electricity, producing only dullness of spirit.

Having no question, there was no answer.

The armchair Vortex of Comrade Spike drained goodwill from the day. The silence deepened. Like a thousand graves sat The Milligan. If it had been Remembrance Day, it could not have been more quiet. I heard the faintest whirring of the camera as time passed. Then time stopped.

Spike sat there, deep in his chair, staring malovently at the interviewer, waiting for a question. Any question. I have never seen him so still. Opposite him, the man's smile was frozen. God knows how many centuries later he shook himself and announced:

'Well… That was Spike Milligan, in town this week. And as far as I'm concerned, the sooner he gets out of town the better! Good riddance, Spike Milligan!'

Spike lurched out of the studio. I stayed behind a moment to offer my own services, hoping to make a few bob, but not surprisingly this overture was rejected.

The event (which I would call An Experiment In Time) was not broadcast.

Terry Wogan, you never had it so good.

I did not see Spike much for the next couple of years. I was drinking heavily, living in Cornwall, making forays to London to let people know I was an Important Figure on the theatrical scene. But the gig was nearly up.

I did make a brief TV appearance when I broke into a BBC studio during a live broadcast – a comedy symposium of famous writers of the day – and from the back declared, 'I am the victim of political exclusion!'

The floor manager crawled along the back of the podium, clutching at my trouser leg, asking me to leave, and as I had not prepared a speech – doing the whole thing impromptu – and had run out of steam, I allowed him to lead me off.

BBC 2 showed the incident as part of their 25th Anniversary celebrations, but as I was not paid in the first place, no repeat fee was forthcoming. People like a bit of entertainement, don't they? Writer as nutcase. The Public used to visit mental asylums for a day out.

Speaking of which, I was in and out of various puzzle factories, drying out, and stayed in one long enough to receive a solicitous letter from Spike. He would always champion the under-dog and do what he could to help the mentally sick. I qualified on both counts.

When it seemed all up – I was back in Cornwall, my wife caring for me – I received on the same day, our wedding anniversary in April '68, two pieces of good news... The Royal Court Theatre had accepted my play Trixie and Baba for main house production, and The Bedsitting Room film rights were sold, with Richard Lester set to direct.

At last there was something to celebrate. More drinking, of course.

It was arranged that I write the screenplay and, God knows how, I managed it. It's true that I did write while I was in the depths of alcoholism but, for others to suggest that to heal an artist of his sickness may heal him of his talent, is unmitigated bollocks. We have a right to be human – even a genius has a right to look himself in the mirror in the morning – it's called human dignity – and, no apologies, if the world loses a talent thereby, well, perhaps one man has found his soul.

I know what is more important. Get the priorities right. It will all sort out.

Begone tortured artist! Poor performing bear…

(No more ears in the post, Van Gogh, thank you!)

With my family, my wife and three children, we moved back to London, into modest rented accomodation. The £2,500 for the screenplay did not go far (and the two and a half per cent producer profits of the film came to nought). However I could no longer claim that professional neglect was the root of my troubles.

It was when I was attending rehearsals of *Trixie and Baba* – my fondest dream come true, to be a Royal Court Writer – and I could not look the actors in the face but found myself crying in the toilet – that it hit me, something else was wrong with my life. It was an inside job.

Shortly after that a doctor recommended I seek help for alcoholism. The word had been spoken. I had thought till recently that all else in the world was my problem and that's why I drank. But the doctor suggested it could be the other way round. I did not protest the issue long.

On 17 December 1968 I began a new life of sobriety among others of similar determination, and through the grace of God I have not picked up a drink of alcohol since that day. I have remained clean and sober.

Do not believe the reports of the glamorous life of an alcoholic. I would not trade my best day drinking for my worst day sober.

What's such fun about alcoholism? It's a disease like tuberculosis, or cancer. It's corrosive for all that dignifies a human being. But if it was the only way to get here, I accept that it was the best thing that happened to me.

So, what's next?

PART III

JESUS LIVES IN WANDSWORTH

'Be ye renewed by the renewing of your
    mind.'

St Paul

'But I've lost my mind.'

Milligan

'Next Question…'

St Paul

```
Clerk (me): Name?
Jonah (Spike): Jonah.
Clerk: Occupation?
Jonah: Prophet.
Clerk: Previous employment?
Jonah: Nil.
Clerk: Tottenham Hotspur?
Jonah: Three.
Clerk: Would you be willing to travel to work?
Jonah: As long as I didn't arrive, yes...
Clerk: Place of birth?
Jonah: Tree.
Clerk: Have you any special skills?
Jonah: Yes, I can squeeze into very small cupboards and
whistle 'Ave Maria' standing on one leg, but I haven't
found much call for this.
Clerk: Will you take any employment that is offered to you?
Jonah: Could you rephrase that question...
Clerk: Yes, is that employment any you to offered with you?
Jonah: Evasive answer. Shuffles feet and deals them.
Clerk: So you refuse to work?
Jonah: Yes, on religious grounds...
Clerk: Like what?
Jonah: Like a church cemetery...
```

From 'Jonah', *The Milligan Papers.*

I'm a bright shiny new-minted Nut Case, still only thirty-five years old... and where was Spike? Where did he crop up next in my life?

Ah, there you are, Spike. Coming out of your office. You drop some money on the pavement.

'It's meant to be there,' you say, and keep on walking to your car.

'What do you want, John?'

'I've come to see you.'

Spike reads my T-shirt, 'Jesus Lives In Wandsworth' and laughs.

'And now you've seen me what do you think?'

'It's a nice experience. Jesus loves you,' I added.

'Are you going through a religious phase?'

'I must be. God bless you, Spike.'

The sun shone on both of us and birds sung on telegraph wires.

'My father has a book of British birds,' I declared.

'Do the birds know they're British?' asked Spike.

'The sparrows probably.'

'I have a Book of Famous British Disasters,' said Spike.

'My father would ban that from the house,' I said, breathless as we reached his mini, parked under a cherry tree flecked with blossom and bird droppings.'

'Get in,' said Spike.

'Where are we going?'

'I don't know. Somewhere else.'

So he drove us somewhere else.

'This is it,' said Spike. He parked the car and we entered through the gates of the Brompton Cemetery. It was an untidy mess. It looked as if the dead looked after it. Not so much litter – though there was some of that – as overgrown grass, bushes, weeds, hiding white flashes of tombstone, a glimpse of marbled hall, an angel shouting through a branch, 'Over here!'

The dead had set up residence in a big way, then let it all go to seed. Once they were respectable, cut lawns, fresh flowers, polished brass urns, and polite stone angels who never said a word. Not now…

'Fuck,' said one.

'Well,' I said. 'It's pretty quiet here.'

'If the dead were noisy there would be no place to go,' uttered Spike. 'It's my last hope.'

'That angel just swore,' I said.

'Which one?'

'The one with the broken trumpet. He is sounding The Resurrection of the Dead. One day he will call them back to Life Eternal.'

'He'd be useless at Ronnie Scott's, by the look of him,' said Spike.

Spike is restless. The angels are moving. Ganging up on him. That's what he feels.

'Then why come here?'

'Because I want to face it here.'

He looks at me and smiles. And relaxes.

'You are so much better without the drink. I told you it changed your personality. You became like Johnny Speight. It's alright for him…'

'What?'

'Being Johnny Speight. It suits him. But you're better off being John Antrobus, believe me.'

'I don't know who he is.'

'Then stop looking…'

Spike is sitting on a tomb, legs dangling. He is quite bemused by the new me.

'So you want to be like Jesus now? Instead of Johnny Speight?'

'Well, Jesus with laughs.'

'Be yourself. That's hard enough.'

A rhododendron flared in the sunlight. The atoms danced. I could see right through them. Spike continued, 'If Jesus was alive today he'd be hopelessly lost. He'd be wandering around wearing a T-shirt with John Antrobus Lives In Wandsworth written on it. He was neurotic. He wanted to save the world. It's not worth saving.'

A tug of wind threw petals in the air and Spike caught one.

'Jesus couldn't save the world. He couldn't even save Kensington Town Hall today. Because the property developers are moving in. With their demolition balls. You can't stop them. They're destroying everything in London that Hitler missed.'

'I wonder if Goering was subcontracting the Luftwaffe to them,' I mused.

Spike laughed.

'What do you believe in, Spike?'

'Me.'

'Is that enough?'

'Probably not. But it's all I've got. Look we're all the same as Jesus. So you might as well get on with being yourself because that's the only way you're ever going to be like him.'

An angel reading a scroll cast in granite until the cows come home, muttered:

'Codswollop.'

'Strange place this.' I shivered.

Spike stood up. A cloud crossed the sun. He threw away the petal and watched it flutter to the ground joining the crimson carpet.

'Everything is alive,' he said. 'Jesus was right. One day the very stones will cry out, but this lot won't hear them.'

'They're stone deaf,' I said.

'If Jesus was working for the BBC,' said Spike, 'he wouldn't need a crucifixion. He'd be suffering enough already.'

The angels laughed and we went home. That was a day that didn't go wobbly with the trees curling up like a Van Gogh painting, the sky a darkening whirlpool and marble mausoleums crashing in on us.

The missile sped to the wall and hit it with a

PLOP

gathering kinetic energy then whizzed back into the badminton court. Spike flailed at the ball with his racquet and miraculously got a hit. The ball bounced off three walls. I rushed forward and with a deadly drop shot killed the point.

'Well played, Somme Company!' Spike called out, doing his General Montgomery impression.

'Thank you, sir!'

In our minds we were at the Royal Military Academy, Sandhurst. I was reincarnated as Officer Cadet Antrobus.

'Shall I introduce the exploding ball on my next serve, sir?'

'Yes, but mind the shrapnel.'

My brilliant foray early in the game was not to be repeated. Milligan played badly and won. I could give him a good game which meant I was appalling to his bloody awful. But we had great fun and played badminton as often as twice a week at the club in Westbourne Park Grove.

When Spike heard noise coming through the walls from the adjoining courts he would shout out:

'Be quiet! There are people in here trying to sleep!'

In the changing room Spike is chatting to some blokes about rugby and Ireland's recent defeat by England, by some monstrous score like 47 points to nil.

'Ireland were very lucky to get nil,' explained Spike. 'Mind you. When the team got back to Dublin there were big celebrations.'

'Why's that?' asked a naked gent, towelling his nuptials vigorously.

'Because they're no good at arithmetic,' said Spike, laughing like a madman.

I followed him into the shower.

As the waters poured upon us. I shouted, 'That was a jolly good game, sir! Thank you!'

'Yes, it was!' Spike as Monty.

'Do you think we'll ever invade China, sir?'

'Not really! The cat's scratched up the map!'

'Anyway we're quite friendly with the Chinese today, aren't we, sir?'

'Yes, I've been there! I saw them in the showers! A fine body of men! Not like this lot! Held together by varicose veins, they are! If their wives weren't so ugly, their marriages would fall apart.'

We left the shower after a cold douche, towelled off, dressed and drove back to the office at Orme Court in Spike's Mini which rattled with loose change.

He was ready. He could have fed a thousand parking meters.

Spike and I decided to write another stage play and Bernard Miles at the Mermaid was keen enough – he would have staged Spike reading a telephone directory, he was not exactly text driven – so he commissioned *The Incurables*.

The story we took was from an unpublished novel (of the same name) I had written in 1968. I had sold the film rights to Apple, the Beatles company. And one day I met with Dennis O'Dell, Sean Connery and Joe McGrath at the premises in Baker Street. This had been a Beatles enterprise, a shop now abandoned and hardly auspicious for our meeting. We walked around the looted show-rooms in the vain hope of picking up a piece of bric-à-brac, a souvenir from the lost empire of Beatles mania and psychodelic days but all that was left was a scattering of uninteresting coat hangers.

Connery had read the book and was interested to play the lead, the mad policeman, Inspector Hedge, who believed everyone else in his division hated him and were out to get him.

The Inspector is sent on a case to investigate a murder in an incurable ward – they have a disease that will kill them off in a few weeks – and our hero points out to his superintendent the futility of the exercise. They will all be dead soon enough, so who cares who kills who? Besides which it's dangerous interviewing subjects. Bedside encounters during which the Inspector will be wearing a decontamination suit.

'Look, justice must be seen to be done, or else it's a farce,' insists the Super. 'We cannot let them murder each other with impunity.'

The Inspector reluctantly accepts the assignment. In the ward he is deliberately contaminated with the disease and joins The Incurables, given a pair of pyjamas and a bed. The Super visits and through a well protected glass screen lets the Inspector know that enough is enough – they've lost one of their best men – the Yard is dropping the case. Goodbye. Inspector Hedge decides to continue the case on his own... (Sounds good. Must reintroduce to publisher. J.A.)

The Incurables story took a different turn when Spike and I started work on it. Suddenly it was World War Two, 1940, later to be known as 1941.

A group of government scientists had been working on a new secret weapon, the Prune Bomb. The explosive power of dried prunes had long been known.

'Brown Power!' shrieked The Milligan and fell tormented beneath his desk. He arose as an impersonation of Winston Churchill and addressed his aide, General Alanbrooke.

'Harness the awesome power of the vast unused stock of NAAFI dried prunes into one devastating bomb, Brooky.'

'Yes, sir. Immediately, sir.'

'Drop Mulberry Harbour, it will never work.'

'Yes, sir.'

'And stop being a yes man.'

'Yes, sir. I mean no, sir. Right, sir. Yes, sir.'

'Drop this dried prune bomb on the Third Reich with a gigantic...'

Spike blew his best raspberry yet.

Alanbrooke, said, 'I'll open a window, prime minister.'

'Don't worry, it's one of ours,' said Spike and fell off his chair, clutching his stomach with laughter.

Unfortunately the secret government experiment went wrong. Someone dropped a test-tube and the scientists contracted a deadly disease, code name Green Swan. They were isolated in a nissen hut on the Duke of Hamilton's estate in Scotland.

The plot thickened as Rudolph Hess parachuted in seeking an armistice with the British Government and a mission to get medicines for the Führer at Boots, Piccadilly Circus. Hitler relied on a regular supply of Galloways lung syrup to keep going. Also Goering needed pile ointment. And where was Lord Halifax to discuss peace terms?

Hess had stumbled into the highly contagious hut of the The Incurables. He was directed by the nurse to get ready for bed.

'You'll find some clean pyjamas on that patient over there.'

But Hess, Third Reich No. 2, would have none of it.

'I always sleep in our National Flag to the Music of the Valkyries,' he insisted.

The Incurables, who were not having a good war, surrendered immediately to Hess.

'What about the others?' he demanded.

'Ah, you mean the British Empire?'

'No, the Golders Green Empire! It must be demolished. And on the site the Führer will build a factory for the production of flashers waist-high practise mirrors! We are not fools! Look at this…'

He produced a garlic sausage.

'It's a sausage.'

'To you it is a sausage, to me it is an Armistice.'

We got half way through the first act then inexplicably stopped. Why? Did we start trying to make sense of it? That would have been fatal.

Spike gave up on the project. The joy for him had disappeared.

'Take it, John. It's yours. Do what you like with it.'

I produced a version but Bernard Miles turned it down. Without Spike to appear in it he was no longer interested and gave the impression he had not even read the script.

'If Spike don't like it, this dog won't wag it's tail,' he said with simple country wisdom.

There was a happy resolution to this story when in 1986 I wrote a radio series for Spike, called *The Milligan Papers*. Six half-hour shows. Two of the shows told the story of *The Incurables* and Spike happily played Hess, and not Winston Churchill but his Chief of Staff, General Alanbrooke.

(*The Milligan Papers!* Buy the CD from BBC Enterprises, folks! And help a Republican enjoy his royalties!)

It's 1972.

Or it's now and I am writing about 1972.

Or it's now and you are reading about what I wrote about 1972.

I have written a new play for the Royal Court in three days flat, *Crete And Sergeant Pepper*. Bill Gaskill, the chap I mentioned earlier, is now Artistic Director and magically he was on the phone a few days after I sent it in.

'Yes. We love it. We'll take it.'

Spike came to audition for two parts, Major Crouchley-Smythe and Sergeant Billings. As Milligan was known to be mercurial, Peter Gill the director – with all due reverence and respect – had asked if the Great Man would consider reading the roles.

Spike could be quite simple, unaffected, not bothered about His Image, darling. He turned up like a jobbing actor in his Trotsky cap, did comrade Milligan. And so did quite a crowd to watch him grace the main stage of The Court.

In 1941 the British army was sent to Greece to help repel the invading Nazis. They arrived in time to join the disastrous retreat from the Northern front. The RN was waiting to evacuate the army from beaches in the south.

Sergeant Pepper, in a moment of panic, orders five rounds rapid fired at Major Crouchley-Smythe, and the clerical section leave their officer for dead with a big iron safe containing the regimental papers. They escape to Crete with other remnants of the defeated army.

The Battle for Crete follows. Germany wins, Britain grabs a silver and Australia is disqualified.'

In the POW camp, while waiting for transportation to the Third Reich, the clerical section are embarrassed when Major Crouchley-Smythe turns up at the gate, a blood-stained bandage round his head, and with four German soldiers carrying the safe...

PEPPER: How did you get off the beach, sir? With the safe
and all?
SPIKE as MAJOR: It's a complete blank, Sergeant - but when
I remember I'll remember in triplicate. That's a joke,
Sar'n.
PEPPER: Thank you, sir. Permission to laugh?
MAJOR: I don't blame you and your men for abandoning me
when you thought I was dead. Struck by a Hun bullet. But
now we must take the regimental papers back to Cairo where
the regiment is being reformed.

PEPPER: The Crout won't let us go to Cairo, sir.

MAJOR: We break out. Escape.

PEPPER: With a bloody big safe? Oh, you mean take the papers from the safe, sir?

MAJOR: Certainly not. You can't take the papers from the safe, man. Without a signed chit from the CO - and the new CO is in Cairo reconstituting the regiment - and what good is a regiment without its regimental papers? Have you got no sense of regimental history, Sar'n Pepper? In that safe are ammunition returns from the Battle of Balaclava - sick reports from the morning of the Battle of Waterloo - and two court-martials from the Battle of the Marne! The regiment has been decimated from time to time, yes, but down through the years we have passed on a thread of administration, a piece of red tape, eh, that's held intact, come what may - the soul of the regiment!

PEPPER: Sir! Yes, sir - but men's lives...

MAJOR: You can't burn men's lives - but you can burn paper! The Hun will strike a mortal blow once he gets that safe open. They know the value of good administration. That is how they hope to win the war. Admin. Red tape. Bumph! But I've told the Hun. They cannot open the safe without a chit. So they're stuck for the moment, cabling Berlin for further orders.

PEPPER: Yes, sir.

MAJOR: We must get the regimental safe to Cairo.

PEPPER: How?

MAJOR: Disguised as a tin of spam. That's another joke, sergeant. You see how British humour transcends class, so that we all join in the fun?

PEPPER: Yes, sir. Thank you sir. Ha, ha, ha, sir.

Milligan caught the meanly Mad Major perfectly – who was trying to lure his section back to Cairo for a court-martial for attempting to kill their officer. Or was he? Better to kill him and make a good job of it this time.

On to Sergeant Billings, a born-again Christian, who was saving up water, scarce in the camp, in an old tin bath to totally immerse converts. He was also carving the Sermon of the Mount on a cherry pip.

Before the demented Major had turned up, Sergeant Pepper had gone to see Billings, seeking absolution for killing his own officer.

PEPPER (*Approaching*): Hello, Billings!

SPIKE as BILLINGS: Blast! I shall have to start again. Creeping up on me...

PEPPER: Why? Why do you do it? Carve the sermon of the Mount on a cherry pip? A plum stone would be better, you know... Can't you get hold of a plum stone? I could maybe get you one...

BILLINGS (*Examining cherry stone with bit of broken glass*) No, I can't go back - blessed are the peace makers - the 'K' trails there - blessed are the peace makers - I got that far - Damn and blast you, Pepper! I can't go back! Blessed are the Peacemakers for They are the children of God! I must go on...

PEPPER: A trailing 'K' won't hardly notice.

BILLINGS: Every blemish must be accounted for.

PEPPER (*Stares at pip*): I can't see nothink - I can't see nothink on it.

BILLINGS: You need to look at it with this bit of broken bottle.

PEPPER: I'm not screwing any broken bottles into my eyes...

BILLINGS: Here...

PEPPER (*takes glass - studies cherry stone*): This stone belongs to Sergeant Billings.

BILLINGS: That's correct, yes - well, I don't want anyone getting it mixed up...

PEPPER: There's a lot of cherry stones around this time of year... Oh, I've dropped it...

BILLINGS: You great clod. That's three months' work...

PEPPER: Oh, dear. Yes... no... Here it is.

BILLINGS: Give it here...

BILLINGS (*takes it and studies it*): You bloody fool, that's a piece of rabbit dropping.
PEPPER: I could have sworn there was some writing on it.
BILLINGS: Oh, aye - this dropping belongs to Brer Rabbit... You are forgiven, Pepper.
PEPPER: What, for losing your cherry pip?
BILLINGS: For everything, man. That's what you've come for, isn't it?
PEPPER: Even for killing a man? One who's on your own side?
BILLINGS: It's easier to kill him. You know his faults... All is forgiven, Sergeant Pepper.

'Thank you very much, Mr Milligan!' called Gill, from the auditorium. 'That was brilliant!'

Which it was.

Spike screwed up his eyes against the light and spoke into the darkness of the stalls,

'Shall I give up my day job as a jelly wobbler?'

We never cast Spike, much as he was loved. And brilliant and touching in the reading. The fear was he would go down-hill from there – improvising and losing the thread of the character. Today I can say we should have taken the chance. He might well have stayed within the orbit of his part. After all, Spike was a reasonable man, wasn't he?

No.

So that was that.

I said, 'Spike, you didn't get the part.' He said, 'That's alright, John. As long as you didn't give the role to Peter Sellers, I'm not jealous. I'll keep writing.'

Spike was always writing.

'Why do you write so much?' I asked him. 'What motivates you? Love of words?'

'The words I love most,' said Spike, 'Are when my bank manager says Mr Milligan your current account is in credit.'

'But you're already a National Institution,' I said.

'Yes, like Wormwood Scrubs. If I get too famous they'll pull me down and build a branch of Sainsbury's.'

'It's true the world's love is fickle,' I sighed.

'I hate them,' said Spike.

'What, mankind?'

'Yes.'

'That's a lot of people. How do you find time to hate them all?'

'I start with the Inland Revenue and hope they'll tell the others,' said Spike. 'The human race is finished. They came last.'

Spike asked me, 'Would you like to come to the Albert Hall, John?'

'Why should I?'

'I've got a box for the Last Night of the Proms.'

It was a glorious occasion.

Spike was in a dinner jacket with a red rose in the buttonhole. Friends and family filled the box. Someone below looked up and pointed. . .

'There's Spike Milligan!'

'There's a twit!' shouted Spike, pointing back.

He surveyed the scene. 'This crowd has come straight from Twickenham. They won't be satisfied unless it's the London Symphony Orchestra, 43 – Beethoven Nil. I'm glad Ireland aren't playing Vivaldi, they'd be sent off.'

There was a fair sprinkling of Union Jacks being waved but the atmosphere was yet to build.

'Up the Irish!' shouted Spike.

Cheers.

The orchestra drifted in and took their places. There were a few whistles and cat-calls. Then a hush of expectation descended on the audience.

'The conductor is coming on, Daddy,' said Jane.

'Pause while he puts in his ear-plugs,' commented Spike.

The conductor strode to the podium and ignoring the audience, tapped his music stand to make sure it would not fall over. He waited for silence to descend, meanwhile turning a page in front of him.

'He's checking his bank statement,' said Spike. 'He's on an hourly rate so he'll be conducting very slowly tonight.'

We burst out laughing. The conductor spun round, his hair an orb of curls framing his refined features.

'Ladies and gentlemen,' he announced. 'I hope you all enjoy immensely this evening's proceedings. We hope to be found not guilty and will be passing round the hat after the performance for the coach driver. Thank you.'

It was a festive night of music. A celebration of life. Foreign tunes and English patriotism. We won, of course. Aided by The Milligan who produced his own baton and conducted as first reserve.

Afterwards the Milligan party went to The Trattoo off Kensington High Street. Alan Claire, an old friend of Spike's (I knew him from *Bedsitting Room* days), was playing the piano at the restaurant.

'You're still alive then,' Spike joshed his pal.

'I fear not, Spike. My wife has booked my funeral because she wants to get it out of the way before Christmas.'

A trumpet was produced from somewhere and Spike, who still had the lip for it, put in a handsome though short-lived performance.

'Gawd, it takes it out of you,' said Spike, breathlessly. 'I'll have to stop shagging my wife.'

'You could stop shagging mine if you wanted to cut down,' suggested Alan.

'Aren't you scared to put the next word down? Sometimes? Don't you wonder if what you are doing is not working, Spike?'

'No. I'm too busy to be scared. Life is too short. There are too many interruptions. I am an endangered species of one. I hope for the children who can see the light. But they grow up and disappear, to be replaced with blank-faced walls on which can be pasted slogans.'

'Like, "Save the Black Rhino",' I suggested.

Spike smiled. 'I love you, John,' he said. 'Don't give up. Don't become like the others. The Great Undead.'

In Spike's office I would meet a various assortment of people. Michael Foot, for example, a calm man with a cutting intelligence, a dedicated parliamentarian. Spike (though suspect was his love for the masses) wrote occasional articles for *Tribune*, which Michael was then editing.

They were both involved in the Campaign For Nuclear Disarmament. On one of the four-day marches from Aldermaston, Spike joined the marchers at Kensington High Street and nobly walked to Trafalgar Square where he gave a rousing speech. I asked him why he had not marched farther.

'I'm not the poor bloody infantry,' he replied. 'I'm Royal Artillery. I skivved off all the marches I could in the war, I'm not going to start now.'

I did not mean to catch Spike on the raw.

'I don't need to march for four days to prove I care,' Spike went on. 'I care about saving beautiful buildings from the property developers, how many days do I march for that? I care about animals and animal experiments – I care about the population explosion – but if I spent all my time marching for everything I care about, I'd be so exhausted I WOULD'NT CARE ABOUT ANYTHING. I'd just have fallen arches.'

'Before the property developers knocked them down,' I said. 'You're excused boots, Spike, don't worry. Plimsolls on parade.'

Spike forgave me. 'You could go and get some jam doughnuts, John.'

'Your favourite,' I said. 'How many each?'

'Three. They provide energy for the brain. Do you know how many calories we burn off thinking?'

'No idea.'

'Nor have I. Get seven. Just in case.'

'In case what?'

'In case I stop thinking. Then you can give me the extra doughnut.'

'The aim of meditation is to stop thinking. All we'd have to do is stop eating doughnuts and we'd enter a state of nivana. Sheer bliss.'

'Sheer bliss is eating jam doughnuts,' said Spike. He thrusts some notes and change into my hands.

'That's more than enough,' I said.

'Buy some clean underwear in case you get run over on the way back.'

'Will you come looking for me?'

'No, I'll come looking for the doughnuts. If they've been run over I'll visit them in hospital.'

'Will you take them some grapes?'

'No, I'll take them some doughnuts.'

Once at a party when Michael Foot arrived, Spike announced, 'Ladies and Gentlemen, Britain's next Prime Minister!' We all clapped the aspiration but fortune telling was to prove not one of The Milligan's outstanding talents.

Then there was Father O'Malley, a reformed whisky drinking priest, who turned up one day in Spike's office.

'I used to preach hell-fire and damnation,' he explained. 'I don't know who else was scared but I terrified myself. I was in Africa. I would sail through the most dangerous road blocks standing up in the back of the jeep holding up the cross! The soldiers could see I had no fear and imagined, no doubt, it was the Holy Spirit. But it was Johnnie Walker!'

'Where did you meet Spike,' I asked the beaming priest, who was prone to peals of laughter which set us all off.

'I was in a retreat for similarly afflicted priests – a good subject, Spike, if I might say so for a comedy – when I came across Puckoon. Such did it delight me and cheer me up that I wrote a word of thanks to the author. Who now stands before me, resplendent…

'In his Derry & Toms underwear,' said Spike. 'Father O'Malley has bought a race horse.'

'It's only got three legs. It always loses. It only once won a race and that's when I lost a fortune. Unpredictable beast!'

'Poor Father O'Malley,' giggled Spike. 'He was flogging the lead from his own church roof in Donegal.'

'Only because I didn't have a pot to piss in, Spike. A body must needs eat or there's no housing for the spirit. Sure the congregation were very good about it. When the rain leaked upon the righteous they wrote to the bishop demanding a new roof.

Blaming the tinkers. They'd taken everything else, hadn't they just? But I got the lead before them!'

'Your congregation must have cared about you,' I ventured.

'Oh, they did. I told them straight it is more blessed to forgive than be forgiven. And I gave them three winners for Punchestown. Ah, the whole thing blew over. Sure we're only human. Why pretend otherwise?'

We went to lunch at Bertorelli's in Queensway. Father O'Malley, like me on the wagon, refused to have his wine glass filled.

'How do you manage communion?' I enquired.

'Mass, you mean? Well, I used to drink up the rest of the wine and make sure there was plenty of it. That way I didn't have to hide bottles round the church. Where there's a will there's a way.'

'Isn't gambling a substitute for drink?'

'I damn well hope so,' roared the priest, merrily, 'or there'll be nothing to keep me in this world. My God, I need a winner!'

'How about saving souls?' spluttered Spike between waves of laughter.

'Much over-rated. My God, teaching people to be human is hard enough…'

'What about the after-life?'

'Well, if you're throwing this life back in God's lap with a miserable face, what right have you to expect another?'

'Do you have confidence in the resurrection?'

'I do. Didn't I get sober? That was a resurrection of sorts. Never mind the after life, stay away from the first drink and you can't have the others.'

'Just for today,' I said. I guessed where Father O'Malley went for help.

'Do you believe in Jesus?' I asked. I had long since given up wearing my Jesus Lives In Wandsworth T-shirt.

'I do. My God, I'm not taking money under false pretences. Of course I believe in Jesus. It's part of my job description.'

Spike said, 'Jesus was inconsistant. He said he who has seen me has seen the Father.'

'Oh, yes, that was a shocking thing to say, Spike. Upset the religious nobs of the day, it did. But then he taught us to say the

"Our Father", didn't he? A beautiful prayer, if I might advertise for a moment.'

'So is there a Father, or isn't there?'

'Oh, there is. But it's only a figure of speech to the child in us. Not a physical manifestation. We are the manifestation of the Father, as Jesus said.'

'I regard him as the first atheist,' said Spike. 'Calling us to be his brothers…'

'Or sisters,' I interjected.

'And even if he did believe in a loving Father he felt forsaken on the cross.'

I looked from Spike to Father O'Malley for the answer.

'I'm glad I'm not paying for this lunch,' said the priest. 'Sure it's hard to be convincing without the bottle sometimes. I had more success as a whisky priest in the Belgian Congo than I'm having in Bayswater today. If you want to be converted, it will happen. And if you don't want it, it's still as likely to happen. I'll tell you one thing, my religion didn't get me sober, but sober I can practise my religion.'

Father O'Malley did not (wisely) seek to answer all the theological or polemical questions we fired at him that day, but his simple goodness was a reassurance.

Being Father O'Malley was enough.

Then there was Bombardier Bill What'shisname who burst into the office one day his arms spread wide.

'Spike! My old mukka! My old darling! How are you? Spike Milligan! Bombardier Milligan! What? This man. This man came under fire to come out after me. No man's land… Spike! What? You don't forget something like that. How are you, my old darling? My old love…'

Spike returned the huge hug but looked rather bemused.

'Haven't seen you at the regimental reunions, have we? Why's that, Spikey? Too good for us, are you? What? A man who puts me on his shoulders never mind the machine gun fire! Never mind the mortars my old darling! He gets me back to the first aid post! Saved my life! Hero of the Anzio Beachhead! You are looking at him! My God, when I think of it. I wouldn't be out of a job in

Sutton divorcing my wife if it wasn't for this man. If it wasn't for Spike Milligan I wouldn't be standing before you today, gentlemen, without two brass farthings to rub together, homeless, on the streets. God bless you, Spike, is all I can say…'

Spike lent him £50, until the next reunion dinner and the man went away still singing his mukka's praises.

'Should have given him the VC for that day's work! What? An unsung hero! Not in my book he ain't! The Angel of Anzio I call him! Spike Milligan! What a man! A hero…'

After he was gone Spike gently shut the door and turned to me.

'He's bomb happy. I was never on the Anzio Beachhead. I've never seen him before in my life.'

'Goodbye fifty quid,' I said.

'As long as he doesn't come back tomorrow, I don't begrudge him,' said Spike.

That was the last we saw of Ex-Bombardier Bill What's-hisname. Though we did hear some months later that he had phoned Harry Secombe's agent, wanting to be in touch and thank Harry for saving his life at Salerno.

'God,' said Spike. 'What a missed opportunity. I should have given him Secombe's home address. He's got a spare room. He could have moved in.'

Father O'Malley had a dream…

'I was swimming down a river. Beautiful it was. A fine day.
How many miles shall I do today I was thinking when some
people on the bank waved to me. I swam over. What are you
doing, they asked. Swimming, I replied. And what's that?
Why it's what I'm doing. But they did not understand so I
got out of the river and demonstrated to them the art of
swimming and described how joyous is the experience. They
asked me to write a book on it so I did and called it How
To Swim. A lot of people became very excited by this and
formed a swimming club and made me president. But they did
not venture into the water. Instead they moved inland me
with them, to preside so to speak and built a town and at

its centre a swimming club. Fine building it was and no pool though I suggested it would be a good idea. Swimming became an obsession in the town growing all the while though none went back to the river. Nor me. Swimming was celebrated. Hymns were sung to it Sundays and people asked do you believe in swimming? I said it's time to go to the river but they would have none of it. Non-believers in swimming were spurned and even lost job opportunities and housing was allocated to swimming believers by the town council on that basis, though none admitted it. Riots broke out and there was burning in the City which it now was with a cathedral that celebrated swimming. In all this I began to be shunned for all I could do was cry out, swim, swim or ride bicycles, but don't argue about it. Please. But they set fire to my manse – the swimming brigade I believe it was, for I had let them down badly saying why if none of you swim, how can you call yourselves believers. The non-believers are better. One night I crept away from the City. I had had enough and longed to swim myself in the cool delightful waters of the river. To continue my journey, so to speak. I walked to the river past dreary suburbs and smoking chimney stacks and factories, some quite modern but with outlet pipes leading somewhere. At the river at last I stripped off. I had done with human kind that would not swim. So what? I would swim myself and give thanks for this simple pleasure. Why had I ever left the river to convince others I know not and that's true. For now I would drift to the ocean and convince no-one when I rested ashore nor ever again speak of swimming and it's bliss. Dead fish floated on the surface before my eyes. I swear no, I must not, and as I waded in my tears were the purest water. The acid bath the river had become bit into my flesh. I turned to God: was he the Great Swimmer I know not being myself only a simple crawl and sometimes backstroke man. And He said fear not, O'Malley, for you shall dream another river, sparkling and pure and a new country and new people and together you will swim to the ocean. And that was that.'

'Is that true, Father O'Malley?' I asked. 'That you had that dream? Did you really?'

And he laughed and flapped his skirts, had he farted, but he would not answer.

Spike writing. The typewriter clicking maniacally. The waste paper basket over-spilling and balls of screwed up paper littered round his feet. Totally absorbed. The balls of paper rise. The room fills with cast off pages. Work. The typewriter clicks and rattles. Faster and faster as Spike submerges under the tide of revisions. Click–click–clickerty–click–click–rap–a–tap–tap machine gun fire writing take no prisoners Spike. Until he emerges out of his office clutching the finished script, paper balls rolling on to the landing and shouts:

'It's done! I'm going home!'

Or

'Find me a demo! I'll make a speech!'

Or

'Who needs money? Poor world. Put out a saucer of money!'

Or

'Crickey, I'm alive! It feels good. Pity it won't last…'

He was riding a switchback of emotion. 'Manic-depressive' he would eventually label it. Plaster it on the door of his mind. He helped others of the same affliction and was helped by doing so.

He was the Grand Old Duke Of York,

'And when he was up he was up,

And when he was down he was down,

And when he was only half way up

He was neither up nor down.'

Sign on Spike's door:

DO NOT DISTURB. I'M DISTURBED ENOUGH ALREADY.

The BBC buy my TV play, *An Apple A Day*. Again. Having commissioned it before, then refused it. When Peter Sellers says he wants to be in the play, everyone at the Beeb is on their toes. It's all systems go!

At the last minute Sellers drops out. Not available. Not atypical…

This leaves the Head of Light Entertainment, Michael Mills, with a problem but he solves it more than adequately by casting Peter Cook and Dudley Moore. Throw in Spike Milligan for a cameo role. Add a soupçon of Kenneth Griffiths and we have a formidable cast.

First day of rehearsal they turn up for the read through. Peter Cook is first through the door.

Pete (*hopefully*): Am I late?

Director: No, you're early. Among the first.

Pete: Drat! I'll hide in the toilet.

Dudley Moore comes in and points at Peter.

Dud: If I've arrived after Peter Cook, I must be hours late!

Pete: No, I was wretchedly early, Dud. My reputation's ruined.

Dud: You could claim you've arrived late for yesterday's rehearsal.

Pete: How about a big hug, Dudders?

Dud: At this time of the morning? You must be joking!

Pete: Aren't you feeling tactile today?

Dud: Tactile? Certainly not. You'll be wanting hymns next. Guitar playing and dancing in the aisles!

Pete: There's nothing wrong with being happy clappy, Dudley, in this sad world. In this veil of tears. How about at least a manly handshake? I know the tea urn hasn't been round yet, but go on.

Dud: Alright, then. But don't tell the others. They'll all want a shake.

Pete: Have you a fear of social intercourse, my boy?

Dud: I have, rather. Yes…

Pete: It's alright. I'm wearing a contraceptive.

Dud: I expect you are, this weather! It's still a bit nippy…

They shake hands, then fall into each other's arms, giggling. Dudley drifts to the piano to tinkle a few notes and Peter drapes himself across the instrument, smoking languidly.

Pete: Ah, me! Happy days!

Dud: What does it remind you of, Pete? This moment?

Pete: Being locked in a coal cellar with the lights off. But then, most things do.

Spike lollops in and after a few 'hellos' and hugs, Dudley says, 'I like your shirt, Spike.'

The shirt is a heavy cotton blue and white vertical stripe affair.

Spike: I bought it in a charity shop, second-hand. It's actually prison issue. HM Government.

Dud: Oh, it's very artistic, yes. HMG, yes.

Spike: Yes, I wore it to the Royal Academy Summer Exhibition – Varnishing Day…

Dud: Vanishing day?

Spike: No, we were all there. And this bloke comes up behind me, claps me on the shoulder and says, Parkhurst '68! I said no, Oxfam 1970. How did you get out? he said. I took a mind-altering pill, I told him.

Pete: Did you get a picture in last year's show, Spike?

Spike: Yes I did, Peter. Under an assumed name. Prince Charles put me up to it. He said they're very prejudiced against famous names at the R.A. He said, 'I got so fed up I changed my name to Tom Eccles and I was hung.'

Dud: Well hung, I hope. I wish him well.

At the siege of the tea trolley Ken Griffiths and Spike discuss the Siege of Ladysmith, both Boer War buffs.

Ken:… Yes, Spike, church bells were rung. There were three cheers in the House of Commons when it was announced by the Prime Minister, 'Ladysmith has been relieved.'

Spike: Yes, very relieved. They cancelled the Poll Tax.

Michael Mills, our producer, calls everyone to attention,

'Ladies and gentlemen! When you've quite finished brown-nosing each other, can we please be seated for a read through?'

For an author this is a thrilling occasion, usually the first time you are going to hear your dialogue spoken – however imperfectly. There is a freshness in a read through, before everyone starts learning their lines, forgetting their lines, blocking their moves and suggesting, 'Don't you think my character would say it this way?'

Suddenly out of nowhere, they assume the authority of A CHARACTER to argue with the author to change the lines. As Joan Littlewood often put it, 'Learn to walk like the character first, darling.'

This cast did not make suggestions. They were too professional. Spike played Mr THRUST, and Peter Cook, Mr ELMWOOD, the fathers respectively of Muriel and Clive...

Peter (*Elmwood*): Arnold... I think it's about time we had a chat about the young couple... After all Clive and Muriel represent the future... They are Tomorrow.

Spike (*Thrust*): Tomorrow's Thursday, early closing...

Elmwood: Precisely... Clive and Muriel are half-day people... when we were young we had a much more definite attitude to life...

Thrust: We hated it.

Elmwood: Yes, it gave us something to live for... today young people are neither one thing nor the other... they're not even the third person... listen to this... I am... You are... He is... She is... you can't say that any more, can you... All you can say is 'I am, you are, he might be, she certainly isn't and what the hell's going on here!' To be frank, Arnold, I'm extremely worried about Clive's genders... he doesn't seem to realise there are two of them...

Thrust: Someone should tell him the facts of grammar...

Elmwood: I've been too embarrassed... but somehow I must have a grandchild... someone to whom...

Thrust: To whom... very good...

Elmwood: To whom I can pass on...

Thrust: The present tense...

Elmwood: No, the wrestling arenas!

Went the day well? Yes.

All trace of this historic recording of *An Apple A Day* seems to have vanished from the face of the earth. Certainly from the BBC archives. If there be a person in Alice Springs, Australia, who recorded the play – please contact posterity c/o the author's publisher. I would be very glad to hear from you.

Spike gave us a lovely performance as Mr Thrust, a man with a nice cough. A real gem. A pearler. There was no studio audience for Milligan to play, so he concentrated on playing his part for a change. To perfection, it must be said. When you subtracted an audience, then you could get a performance from The Milligan.

He turned *Oblomov* upside down, into a riotous vehicle for himself, saving an ailing production and making it into a hit. Previously he had attempted over the months of running to do the same thing with *The Bedsitting Room*. But the production was already a hit. The play suffered as a result. He would adulterate the lines and then say, 'I didn't write this,' to get a further laugh.

It's as well that I was off drinking with Jeffrey Bernard.

Because you could never tell Spike he was wrong... Kenneth Tynan pronounced *The Bedsitting Room* a hit before Milligan ever appeared in it.

Spike often told me how much he hated audiences.

'They'll laugh at anything,' he said and he proved that. Why? When he had such a divine sense of humour. This was the nub of working with him that sometimes proved difficult.

'God, that's a terrible line, Spike,' I'd say.

'Fuck 'em,' he always replied. 'It'll get a laugh. Leave it in.'

He saw himself as Gulliver in Lilliput, a giant being tied down hair by hair by the local inhabitants... and he had nothing but contempt for the small minds of most people. The circle of ignorant people grew and the circle of those worth cultivating diminished – until one day I found myself outside it with the other Lilliputians.

'Ah well, hey hoy, hand me that strand of hair and a stout peg, will you?'

The dichotomy between Spike's amazing talents and his unacknowledged human foibles grew as the years passed. These would make it increasingly difficult to work with him – but for the moment there were still fruitful ventures and happy times to enjoy as the Seventies unfolded.

It's difficult to write in one vein about Milligan and the next moment to be writing the opposite. It is as if I am describing two people. I am not suggesting he was schizophrenic because he was not. But Spike could be amazingly kind, helpful, generous with his time and money one moment, the best companion you could hope for on life's highway – and bloody obnoxious and insulting the next.

He had yet to cast himself in the role of Grand Old Man of Letters who pitched hot tar from his battlements on all who dared approach. Another day the drawbridge would be lowered and he would be sunning himself outside the moat, friendly to all passers-by as he pottered about. Indeed the World's Best Friend.

But one word could change that. Words were powerful in Spike's life. He was the Wizard and he lived in his castle. The castle that words had built. A wrong word would have him back upon the battlements, the sky darkening behind him, raining down thunder and lightning bolts…

'Excuse me? Did I say something?'

PART IV

THROUGH THE LOOKING GLASS

'Do you feel anything?' asked Wallop.
'I'm feeling this banana,' replied Hairy.
'You could eat it.'
'That would reduce my options.'
'And if you don't eat it?'
'Everything is possible.'

The Nature of Inertia
John Antrobus

Churchill (John Bluthal): Right, Brooky... read back that memo.

Alanbrooke (Spike): Urgent that you defend Singapore stroke Tobruk stroke Malta stroke India stroke the cat, stroke Benghazi stroke Rangoon to the last man - and then let me have his name.

Churchill: Now how many of our overseas possessions are left then?

Alanbrooke: Oh, they are all left, sir - but mostly in enemy hands.

Churchill: Brilliant. That's brilliant tactics, Brooky... they'll cut our overheads you see... let the enemy take over a place and run it for us until the war is over - then we'll take it back and send them a bill for the rent... Right send a telegram to the First Lord of the Admiralty. Tell him to sink the Tirpitz... sink the Graf Spee... sink the Bismark... raise the Titanic... and sink the Hood before they do! Now what's the time?

Alanbrooke: I'm sorry that's restricted information. By the way, sir, we delayed the Relief of Tobruk so that it matched the date in your memoirs.

Churchill: Well, of course it had to. I can't keep changing things. I mean we've got to stop sending reinforcements to Singapore - because if they hold out against the Japs, it means I'll have to re-write two whole chapters...

From 'The Incurables', *The Milligan Papers.*

Spike and I talked so much about the Fall Of Singapore – our favourite British defeat, much better than Dunkirk – there were no little boats to get the army off, no bobbing Hastings Bell and welcome aboard, lads – there were instead hordes of drunken deserters on the quayside, armed and dangerous, forcing their way on to the few ships available, knocking civilians aside and suitcases into the water. Mayhem. Rape in the city...

And the Japs had not even arrived on the island. Of this we spoke over various dinners, Spike and I, particularly at the Trattoo, embellishing the stories...

The loss of face and of Empire, the loss of the impregnable island fortress with its big guns pointing out to sea. But the Japs had come overland 'damn them' down through the Malayan Peninsular, through forest marked on British maps 'Jungle Impenetrable' but marked on the maps of a cunning foe 'Jungle Penetrable'. So that's how they had got through!

We had imagined Japanese pilots to be myopic behind bottle lens glasses, steering their planes into mountainsides, what a laugh! Comic Cuts figures... And found this hard to square with the Nippon Air Force being Lord of the skies, raining down death upon us daily, hourly, moment by moment, as we hid under tin hats in hastily clawed out slit trenches.

These and other misconceptions, vanities and a class structure between the officers and other ranks carried into captivity and utter deprivation – this was the grey landscape, remnants of White Supremacy in the Far East never to be restored – the last Fire Sale of Defeats of the Century – give-away, knock-down prices, British Empire going for a song which was definitely not Rule Britannia...

On this Spike and I improvised our tales. Not without sympathy for the men and women caught up in that theatre of war, yet theatre it was our minds turned to... was there an absurd piece to write upon this folly of follies? This Bastion of Empire days, Singapore.

We talked and talked. Changi. Internment. Imprisonment. Fly parade...

Once there were too many flies in the Changi POW Camp and for reasons of hygiene the Japanese Kommandant ordered each prisoner to kill 100 flies daily. There was a fly parade at night and jam jars, tins, bottles with the day's kill were inspected. Sometimes counted. One fly short of 100 and a beating followed. After some time flies became a scarce commodity in the camp. A blackmarket sprang up in dead flies. The Chinese sold them to us across the wire in exchange for watches and rings and even Coutts cheques were accepted to be honoured after the war.

'That was the time I bought 1000 dead flies, old chap. Cornered the market, actually. I was known as "The Fly King",' explained Major Crawley in 1946 to his Mayfair branch, Coutts manager – who had just received the cheque for clearance from a Chinese gentleman.

'You were eating the flies?'

'Oh, no, it hadn't come to that. They were far too valuable!'

Spike, in his version, decided he would visit the compound hospital and persuade a mukka to expose a festering wound to attract flies he could swot.

'Ouch'.

'Sorry, mate. Three more and I've got my hundred quota for today.'

'That's alright then, mate. Go ahead. But use minimum force. No need to squash the fly into me scar, is there?'

One evening, while talking after dinner somewhere in Kensington, engrossed in our subject, our two minds as one – an impossible focus of energy, our fevered imaginations wild on the story – we fell Through the Looking Glass into the war.

We were there on the island of Singapore, February 1942, and the Japs were just across the blown-up Causeway, making ready to invade and finish the campaign. It's an occupational hazard of writers, being overwhelmed by their material. You don't hear much about it and I would not say it happened very often. Of course Vincent Van Gogh disappeared into his own landscape and came back demented. It was that sort of thing. Getting in was easy, but there was no guarantee of getting out again – in any fit state of mind.

We were toiling up the hill towards the Royal Singapore Golf Club. We being the remnants of a platoon, a ragtag collection of tired men led by Bombardier Milligan (Spike to his pals). On the Bren gun were the week-old famous team of Roy Sitwell and Alan Ferguson, still wet behind the ears, off the last boat to arrive with reinforcements, shortly before it was sunk by Zero bombers.

Alan lived in a state of apprehension, mouthing to be word perfect in Japanese, 'I surrender and I am very good at mending bicycles.'

Roy, on the other hand, was a cool customer, a beautiful youth who had turned many a scout master's knees to jelly. He could not conceive of dying and Alan could conceive of little else. Their fame resided in the fact that they had shot down a Jap bomber. Alan said they had not meant to, it was a panic reaction: when the gun jammed, they had pointed it at the sky to avoid hitting the RSM and at that moment a Zero had appeared out of nowhere. He was willing to apologise to the Emperor and spend the rest of his life making wind chimes in Nagasaki.

Then there was Private Eric Dickens, recently busted from sergeant for drunkenness and peeing up the leg of a brigadier whom he mistook for a tree.

'If only the silly bugger had kept moving, I'd have known the difference,' explained Eric who spent all his spare time writing sketches, patter and comic songs for a revue he was planning. He had become separated from an ENSA concert party in India after another drunken binge and a certain Major Fraser had shipped him out to Singapore with instructions to generally cheer people up.

On his own authority Dickens had begun auditioning men from various units and had hired the Adelphi Theatre for two weeks and ordered costumes to be made for Aladdin from his Chinese tailor. He cabled invoices to the War Office and took up lessons on the musical saw, but his return instructions were to disband his company forthwith, as of today's date, due to the emergency – 'just when they needed to have something to bloody laugh about' – and he was transferred to the infantry. He got drunk on the news and busted over the wet leg incident with the brigadier. Hence his arrival with the Ragtag platoon.

'HALT!' Spike shouted out.

As we were already sitting around on the verge of the road, smoking, this order had little effect.

'Your timing's bloody awful, Spike,' said Eric. 'You need anticipation. You said Quick March when we were half way down the street.'

'I'll get the hang of it, don't worry' said the newly promoted Milligan.

He was bombed up country,' said Sitwell.

'He should have had a bayonet up his jacksi,' laughed Dickens. 'Anyone got a fag?' He was always on the scrounge. 'I'm a natural leader of men, that's the difference between me and Spike. I once led thirty men to their death.'

'How was that then? How were they killed?' enquired Bill Partridge, an Aussie of no fixed regiment.

'He bored them to death trying his stage act out on 'em,' said Ferguson.

'Oh, yes? Well, you can write the funny lines in future,' said Eric, always on the lookout for talent.

'Now who can tap-dance round here? I'm on the lookout for a tap-dancer, so don't be shy. Speak up.'

'TAKE COVER!' yelled Spike, and threw himself into a ditch.

All that buzzed in the clear blue sky were a couple of flies.

'He's bomb happy,' said Ferguson.

'He's working his ticket,' said Dickens.

'ADVANCE!' shouted Spike.

'I had an advance of 73 Singapore dollars for the two-week run at the Adelphi,' explained Eric, 'But the War Office cancelled the run. A big mistake in my opinion. Bad for morale. You'll see. We'll lose now...'

They moved on and came out upon the golf links. The turf beneath their boots was springy, soft as a carpet in the lounge of Raffles Hotel. Birds sang as if trained and the crickets chirruped discreetly. Starched triangular flags on unblemished white poles adorned the landscape. All was Immaculate Order, not withstanding the dull explosions of ammunition dumps being destroyed some miles away and a pall of smoke rising from burning oil dumps and rubber stocks in the dockside go-downs.

'Right,' said Spike. 'We'll dig our trench here.'

They unpacked the entrenching tools, fixing the wooden handles into the metal slots.

'Where do we begin?' said Eric. 'What are the parameters of this 'ere trench?'

'Parameters,' said Spike. 'We're not building the Acropolis, Eric.'

'It's temporary, is it?'

'What's the difference between a temporary trench and a permanent trench?' piped up Bill Partridge. 'Technically, I mean?'

'I give up,' said Eric. 'You tell me. Anyone got a fag?'

'Our trench has got to last as long as the British Empire,' declared Spike.

'Then it's temporary,' said Eric.

'Hardly worth bothering with,' said Partridge.

'Smoko!' called out Ferguson, and they lit up again, while Bombardier Milligan paced up and down measuring out the trench.

'We've got a perfect 180° field of fire,' he announced. 'If the Japs come up that hill, they'll have no cover. We'll catch them in the open and mow them down. Then collect their identification tags and write to their next-of-kin.'

'We can't write Japanese,' said Ferguson.

'We can learn.'

'Why are we going to write to the families of dead Japs?' asked Roy. His limbs were marble white and hardly a hair marked them.

'Because we can visit them after the war,' explained Spike. 'Stay with the families and shag their sisters.'

'The ultimate revenge,' uttered Dickens. 'We've shagged our own sisters, why shouldn't we shag theirs?'

'Look, just dig, Dickens,' ordered Spike. 'Don't be bolshie. I've got the stripes. When you've got enough room we'll put the hole in.'

'We didn't bring any holes,' said Roy.

'You forgot to bring the holes?' You're bloody useless, Sitwell!' shouted Spike. 'A trench is no good without a hole! How do we get in it?'

'He's right,' said Dickens. 'Perhaps if we dig around we'll find a hole.'

'I've got a hole in my vest,' said Ferguson. 'You can have that.'

'Start with the hole in his vest,' ordered Spike, 'and make it big enough for all of us to get in.'

'Right,' said Dickens. 'Do as Napoleon says or we'll be stuck outside Moscow all winter.'

'Fags out,' said Ferguson. 'Prepare to dig.'

Having run out of idiot conversation for the time being, someone raised an entrenching tool to strike the first blow upon the green.

'STOP!' A querulous voice carried over the ether waves of the balmy day. 'STOP THAT! Whatever you're doing, STOP IT!'

A short figure in a blue blazer scuttled across the links towards us. As he approached, there could be seen upon his pocket a crested anchor, upon his lips a toothbrush moustache and upon his tie, egg stains.

'I am Captain Thomas, Steward of the Links, Secretary of the Royal Singapore Golf Club. What exactly are you men doing here?'

'We're here because of the war, sir,' growled Dickens. 'Otherwise we'd be home in bed.'

Bombardier Milligan stepped forward and saluted smartly.

'Sir! We have been sent to establish a defensive position on the golf links. To find a commanding field of fire. To dig ourselves in and await further orders, sir!'

Milligan saluted again and knocked his hat off.

'Are you mad?' demanded Captain Thomas, RNVR.

'Yes, sir, definitely,' said Milligan. 'I'm glad you noticed. I'm bomb happy, sir. Could you possibly give me a sick note to see the MO?'

'Dig in on the Ninth Green? You cannot desecrate the Royal Sod!' shouted Thomas, his toothbrush moustache working like a conductor's baton. 'This is Sacred Ground. It has taken fifty years to gain perfection. It is the Eighth Wonder of the World. You might as well advertise in the sky 'The Empire Has Fallen' as strike into this earth! Put up your shovels, chaps. Who gave you this unholy order? What devil's spawn is behind this move?'

Silence from us.

'Have you signed orders, Bombardier? Show them to me.'

'Only verbals, sir.'

'Only verbals! Only verbal orders! Nothing written down to incriminate? No signature then?'

'No, sir.'

'I see. But your men are witness to your orders. And to Him who gave it. With such recklessness. Heedless of the calamity that would surely follow. The word would spread like wildfire through the native population – a trench has been dug on the Ninth Green at the Royal Singapore Golf Club! What can this mean? they'd ask. The desecration of the Royal Sod?'

'Who's the Royal Sod, sir?' asked Dickens, poker-faced.

'You stand upon it, man! One spade struck here into this ground and all is lost! The British Empire will founder! It works by symbols. All is face in the Far East. Lose face and we lose the indigenous Chinese. They'll be laughing at us in their opium dens. And the Indian Army already perverted and poisoned by Nationalist sentiment will throw down their arms and join the Japs. Just to hear word of this GRUESOME ATTEMPT upon the links! Oh, lads, stand firm. See the light. Your orders are rescinded. Now give me the name of the wretched bastard who sent you here?'

'Colonel Harrington.'

'Colonel Harrington? So…' Captain Thomas paced the green. 'Stand your men down, Bombardier, and let them smoke. While I resolve this traiterous matter…'

'The Japs could take this club easily enough, sir. If these slopes are not defended. After that Singapore City lies open before them,' said Spike.

'Stand down your men, Bombardier. Do not concern yourself with the bigger picture. You know not of what you speak. This Colonel Harrington…' Thomas spat the words out venomously. 'He is a member of the RSGC and will be blackballed by the committee next Thursday evening, make no mistake. After that a whispering campaign must suffice. Bestial acts against the men, that sort of thing, it will be done. He shall be brought down, never fear. Colonel Harrington will never get another decent game of golf East of Suez. He will be broken. The women won't touch him. He will resort to boys in desperation…'

Private Sitwell blushed. He would not tell. Colonel Harrington had already been kind to him though Roy was having none of it and had removed the hand from his thigh in the staff car. And asked to be transferred from the driving pool. First day in Singapore too. And put on a Bren gun team with Alan Ferguson who'd lost a mate…

A man called Alf Chapman, that was, who had taken one look at the broken city from the ship's rail, the burning warehouses, black smuts raining down upon his face, the quays thronged with deserters, and cried out…

'Fuck me! They sent us here for the surrender! As if they didn't have enough poor sods to put in the bag!'

He had not even got off the ship but disappeared below and somehow vanished…

The angry blazer containing Captain Thomas, RNVR, retired – retired to the clubhouse, leaving the boys of the Ragtag platoon in disarray.

'Call up RHQ', said The Milligan. 'Tell them we've been molested by an angry Welshman who will not let us proceed with the war.'

Bill Partridge was the radio op. He'd been with us since the Battle for Johore as liaison. His own regiment had been decimated. On their right flank an Indian Brigade had run away despite the Aussies shooting out the tyres of their transport to arrest their panicky departure. What was left of Bill's mob, disillusioned, feeling betrayed 'Where's the bloody air cover?' were making their own evacuation arrangements down on the docks. Private Partridge had come across his 'Pommy pals' in the ensuing chaos of retreat and had decided to stick with them.

'Set's on the blink, Spike,' he announced. 'Perhaps we could phone through from the clubhouse.'

'And have a shower and a five-course dinner while we're about it,' added Dickens.

Spike said, 'It's Members Only up there.'

'Well, it's not a Members Only war, is it?' Dickens said.

'Yes, it is,' said Spike. 'In Kuala Lumpur you couldn't be bombed unless you were proposed and seconded.'

'So who let you in?'

'I got a temporary membership to be blown up by a tank shell,' explained Spike. 'It's for World War Two only. On account of my father being in World War One. But you can't be gassed for the first two years.'

'It's who knows who,' grumbled Dickens. 'Why can't I be blown up and gassed?'

'Because you don't come from a military family, do you?' Ferguson pointed out.

'No, we raised ferrets.'

'Then belt up. Temporary members or full members, what's the difference? What I want to know is how do we get out of the war?'

'You have to put your name down for peace,' said Spike.

'Is there a waiting list?' asked Alan Ferguson, desperately.

Roy smiled, beatifically. 'You never know till you ask.'

A rosy hue lit the evening sky from the blazing fires in the City behind them, vying with the glorious sunset opposite. The platoon sat smoking on the ninth hole, enjoying the fine view. Bill Partridge sat fiddling with the radio set. Briefly, faintly over static, Japanese voices, excitedly… then nothing.

'It's dead as a dodo,' declared Partridge, in the gloaming.

'Someone's got to get down to Colonel Harrington for further orders,' said Spike.

'Mine's a pint of bitter.' Dickens again.

'Well, I'm not going,' muttered Partridge. 'The Red Caps are on the road. They'll let you go up to the front but they're shooting anybody coming down again.'

'We're not deserting,' I said. 'We want further orders so that we can win the war.'

'The MPs won't believe that. They'll think you're mad, kiddo.'

'I'm mad,' said Spike. 'I'll go.'

Although I was Acting Unpaid Lance Corporal, nominally 2IC of the platoon, I went with Spike, to keep him company and watch his back. Dickens took over.

As we walked in the light of a full moon, across the golf links looking for the road and the possibility of a lift, an eerie sound wafted through the night. A sinister wailing that set the hair on our necks tingling.

'Jesus, what's that?' gasped Spike. 'A Japanese sushi warning?'

'No, it's Dickens practising on his musical saw.'

'We could win the war with that,' said Spike.'

We chanced being run over in the blackout, thumbing down a lorry load of cheery Aussies. Having second thoughts Spike said, 'Look, Cobbers, nothing personal but we're kosher. We've got to get back to Raffles Square for further orders.'

'Climb aboard, you Pommy bastards! Leave it to us! We'll get you Limeys there, don't worry!'

We reluctantly climbed into the back of the truck, eager hands hauling us up and were soon being driven through the night singing 'Tie Me Kangaroo Down Boys' and swigging spirits from the plenteous bottles being passed round.

'How do you intend to get past the Red Caps?' I enquired politely.

'Don't worry, Cobber, we've got an arrangement with them...'

The arrangement consisted of revving up and speeding the lorry crashing through the barrier, meanwhile firing several bursts from their Tommy-guns over the heads of the MP's to whoops and catcalls and shrieks of laughter.

'It always works,' said the driver. 'It's good clean fun.'

We were dropped off, grateful not to be under close arrest, in Raffles Square. We waved our friends goodbye.

'They don't like a lot of admin, the Aussies,' said Spike. 'Come on, John...'

We entered the foyer of Raffles Hotel.

'Why are we going in here, Spike?'

'Because Colonel Harrington relocates Brigade HQ to the cocktail lounge at sundown,' explained Spike.

'To confuse the enemy?'

'To confuse everybody.'

A doorman stepped into our pathway. 'Officers Only,' he announced, officiously. 'Can't you squaddies read the sign? It's in plain English.'

'Mind your manners, mate,' answered Spike. 'In plain English I'm warning you I'm mad. Stone bonkers, mate. Dangerous to offend. Liable to bite off ears, mate.'

'He's bomb happy,' I put in. 'Pay no attention to him.'

'I'll pay no attention to him, or you, as long as you get your raggy arses out of here. We can't have you disturbing nice decent people, can we? Now get about your business.'

'My fucking business,' replied Spike through gritted teeth, 'is defending your nice decent people, including fat bastards like you. In fact putting my life on the line so that crawlers like you can lord it over your shitheaps, you lickspittle cheap...'

'Guv'ners lackey!' I supplied.

'GUV'NER'S LACKEY,' yelled Spike, grabbing the door-man's collar. 'Now go and get me Colonel Harrington! Before I put a grenade up your jacksi, mate! And the pin won't be in it, I promise you...'

As luck would have it Colonel Harrington, was passing through the foyer and heard the ruckus.

'If I'm not mistaken that's Comrade Milligan,' said Colonel Harrington to his aide, Captain Witherspoon. They came over, full of interest, to see what was going on.

'He cannot enter, sir,' blustered the doorman. 'It's Officers Only. I told him so, thereupon he became violent...'

'He's been trained to be violent,' observed Colonel Harrington urbanely. He turned to his adjutant. 'Percy, lend him your tunic for an hour or two, there's a good fellow.'

'Rightho, sir.'

Captain Witherspoon took off his tunic and handed it to Milligan.

'Am I being commissioned in the field, sir?' asked Spike, donning the tunic.

'No, you're being commissioned in the foyer. Temporarily for enough time to get pissed, understood? Follow me, Terrance, my boy.'

'Yes, sir.' Spike grinned. Thumbs up.

'What about Lance Corporal Antrobus, sir? You can't leave him outside. He's too good-looking.'

Colonel Harrington gave me an old-fashioneded look.

'You're right. Percy! Deal with it.'

'Yes, sir. Right sir.'

As I was down for OCTU (Officer Cadet Training Unit) and had the word of Witherspoon to verify the fact, I too passed through the hallowed portals of Raffles Hotel to mix with the nice decent people in the lounge bar who were drinking themselves to oblivion, hoping the Japanese would not find them there.

Spike made his report on the incident at the Royal Singapore Gold Club and the fact that Captain Thomas, RNVR retarded, had rescinded the orders to dig fortifications on the Ninth Hole.

'The fascist bastard,' swore Colonel Harrington. 'I'll teach that swine a lesson.'

Captain Witherspoon appeared in the bar, wearing a different uniform jacket.

'Percy!' shouted Harry Harrington. 'Get the map co-ordinates of the R S G C, the Ninth Hole! And order an artillery bombardment upon it at Dawn Plus Twelve, tomorrow. By the time we've fucked up his sacred links, his holy turf, he won't notice the odd trench we care to dig.'

'Rightho, sir,' said Witherspoon, cheerfully.

'By the way, sir, King Knight to Rook Seven.'

Harrington stopped in his tracks, blinked, and said, 'You crafty bugger, Percy. That's checkmate.'

'Yes, sir, I do believe it is.'

'Drinks all round,' ordered the Colonel. 'Here's to our Russian comrades and the defence of Moscow. The Hun shall not pass!'

'The Hun shall not pass!' We reiterated, clinking glasses, and drank strong spirits.

(Colonel Harrington and Captain Witherspoon played mental chess every day and continued to do so throughout their years in captivity, a discipline that doubtless helped to keep them alive).

Colonel Harry Harrington loved his men, equal before not God but Trotsky, and despised the Whitehall Wonders.

'You can't wipe your arse without permission from that lot and it takes six months to requisition a toilet roll.'

Spike did not often get drunk, but it was hard going to stay sober in the CO's company.

'Same again, Terrance?'

'I'd better be getting back to the platoon, sir' said Spike. 'I've got to get the lads off the golf links before the barrage.'

'Lots of time, my boy. No hurry. Enjoy your temporary captaincy. Get them in, Percy.'

'Rightho, sir.'

Percy Witherspoon was highly intelligent, tall, dark, saturnine, loved by the ladies. He had a penchant for the wives of his fellow officers and enjoyed the plotting and secrecy. He spoke Malayan and Chinese fluently. He and Harry Harrington were probably in Army Intelligence, even MI 6.

'What chance have we got in Singapore?' asked Spike.

'The chance to put up a good show, Terrance,' said the Colonel, enigmatically.

'And then?'

'Everyday brings something new, eh, Percy?'

'Look for the miracle, sir.'

'The miracle of turning back the Japs?' persevered Spike.

'The miracle lies in never letting the enemy defeat you. Show them you're the better man, eh, Percy? Under all conditions.'

'Yes, sir. Whatever it takes, sir. I'm sure we'll win through.'

'Spike! We'd better be going. It's getting late.'

I wave my hand in front of Milligan's face. 'Hello!'

Harrington and Witherspoon had drifted away to confer with two Chinese bankers about the disposal of some gold reserves and the flow of drinks had temporarily dried up.

We risked insubordination and did not ask for permission to fall out. Instead, arm in arm, we staggered back through the foyer singing, 'The working class can kiss my arse! I'll shag the foreman's daughter…'

The night air enveloped us in warmth, the fragrant garden blossoms fighting the acrid smell of burning rubber. The rubber won. We hailed a taxi. Out of our own pockets we were paying to go back to the front line. The Ragtag platoon were waiting for further orders. We had till Dawn Plus Twelve to get them off the links.

I realised Spike had drunk too much when he ordered the taxi to stop at a dance hall.

'We've got a couple of hours to kill,' he said, and paid off the taxi.

'Come back at 1 a.m.,' I said, desperately.

'OK, sir. No problem,' said the Chinese driver and drove off into the blackout, never to be seen again.

There was an air raid down at the docks, the nightly raid, to add to the conflagration and deaths – but we turned our backs on the distant flashes and explosions. It was a good time to dance.

The Chinese taxi-dancers were beautiful and patient with our drunken cavorting. We booked the girls per dance and, as can happen in war, fell in love for the night at a favourable hourly rate. It was suggested we go on somewhere.

'No, thanks,' I said.

'We've got time,' said Spike. 'Don't worry.'

'What about the golf links?'

'What about some nooky?' said Spike, michievously.

We left the dance hall and were soon in the erotic lodgings of our Chinese hostesses. They had turned their meters off out of fond fraternal feelings for the soldier boys… but up on the links the clock was still running for the rest of the lads camped beside the Ninth Hole.

'Spike, we must go.'

'Not yet. Suzy and I are going to open a Chinese laundry in Lewisham and wash the grey out. Isn't that good news?'

'Spike, we must go.'

'Not yet…'

We emerged into the pre-dawn of Shanty Town as sober and worried as the two thin mangy cats that mewed at us. We could make it, of course. There were no taxis in sight. We grabbed a passing rickshaw to take us to the main road. From there we were confident – no, not confident, hopeful – that we could thumb a lift.

But once on the road we found little in the way of military transport passing up to the line and the few lorries that lumbered past, their dark shapes becoming ever-more etched against the lightening sky, did not stop.

'We're running out of time, Spike.'

'Don't worry, John. I know what to do.'

As a civilian car – lights dimmed for blackout reasons – approached, Spike leapt out on to the road and pointed his rifle at the windscreen.

'Stop!' yelled Spike.

The car skidded to a halt.

A portly European, probably a rubber planter, angrily wound down his window and drawled drunkenly, 'What the hell…'

Spike pulled the door open and dragged him out.

'Get in the other side, John! Quick!'

I opened the passenger side door and pulled the floozie or wife, whatever she was, out of the car. She screamed and scratched at me with her long painted nails, but I shoved her off the road, into the ditch, and jumped into the car. Spike, meanwhile, hit the man in the stomach with his rifle butt.

'Sorry, pal. Not time for explanations.'

We were on the road, gunning the car away from the couple whose expectation of sexual fulfilment we had spoiled, unless they settled for a quickie in the ditch.

The sky was streaked with crimson, presaging sunrise and a nice spell of weather.

'We're going to make it,' said Spike, determinedly. 'And if we don't, I never did like Dickens.'

'If we hadn't gone to Shanty Town for a shag, we wouldn't be up against the clock now.'

'Don't regret the past, John. You've a right to a shag. You never know when it's going to be your last.'

I said, 'I never know when it's going to be my first.'

Spike slowed the car as we approached a road block. A metal pole barred our way.

'We shouldn't have any trouble getting through,' I said. 'They'll be glad of anyone going up to the front.'

I expected that we would be waved through but the two Red Cap NCOs and the Bastard Red Cap Officer built like a shithouse had something on their minds... so we stopped to explain our orders. They were not really interested in them. What did fascinate them was the fact that Spike was still wearing Captain Witherspoon's tunic.

Bombardier Milligan explained how he had borrowed it for a bevy at Raffles Hotel on the orders of his CO and that we really must go now.

'That's a tall story,' said the burly sergeant. 'Drinking with the CO, eh? Very nice too, if you can get it.'

'You couldn't,' said Spike. 'You're too ugly!'

'Look, phone our CO and verify our orders...'

'We haven't time for that,' Spike interrupted me.

'Get that pole out the way, sarge, and I'll see you get a medal.'

'You said I was ugly...'

'I was playing hard to get. Look, I've got to get my platoon off the golf links.'

'Why, what's their handicap?'

'Their handicap is they don't know they're going to be blown to Kingdom Come in 15 minutes.'

The young broken-nosed Lieutenant, obviously a rugby player, bent over the car and looked hard at Spike.

'This man is impersonating an officer,' he declared in a silly high-pitched tone. His nose was broken but not his voice.

'I don't do impersonations, sir.' said Spike. 'I play the trumpet. For God's sake let us through. We're heading towards the enemy, what more do you want? Just say CHARGE!'

'You've told us a story, soldier, that we're not going to verify – or otherwise – by getting Colonel Harrington out of bed. You're cheeky, but as you're going in the right direction we'll let you through this time...'

The Lieutenant nodded to his Corporal who raised the barrier. The Lieutenant smiled at us, as a tiger might, 'Don't play silly buggers again. Oh, by the way, you'd better give me that tunic, bombardier. Who's it belong to? I'll see he gets it back.'

Spike wriggled out of the tunic and handed it through the window.

'Captain Witherspoon, sir. With my compliments.'

Next thing Spike was dragged from the car and slammed up against the jeep and the two NCOs had their pistols drawn and pointed at him.

'So I was sick on his tunic!' yelled Spike. 'That's not a court martial offence!'

'Captain Witherspoon was found robbed and murdered in his hotel room in the early hours of this morning. You've got some explaining to do, Milligan.'

'Well, if he was robbed after he was murdered, he wouldn't have any use for the stuff anyway,' said Spike with a mad laugh.

I seized the chance while all eyes were on The Milligan and slid over to the driver's seat and accelerated away too quickly for a pistol shot to find its mark.

The sun orbed blood red over the brow of the hill and in twelve minutes the men of the Ragtag platoon would be under a murderous barrage, courtesy of the Royal Artillery...

We were back in the Trattoo, High Street Kensington. Spike was playing the trumpet serenely and Alan Claire was on piano. Shelagh sat contendly sipping a glass of wine and puffing on a fag. Since Spike generally disapproved of her smoking, he must have been feeling indulgent that evening.

I got my bearings – orientation, back from Singapore – it was as if I'd come out of a blackout as I used to in drinking days, latterly, and had no idea where I was or how I'd spent the last half hour. Or was it three days?

I caught Spike's eye and threw it back. Yes, we both loved Stephen Leacock.

The point is that I was trying to establish with Spike a rapport, a secret acknowledgement that we had just returned from a thrilling adventure together but there was no connection. Had I imagined the whole thing?

The evening wound down. All the other customers left –
the Bed Early Brigade – and the waiters began emptying ashtrays
and sweeping the floor and yawning. When they strayed into the
piano area Spike insisted they drink wine with him and the party
was renewed. Shelagh gratefully called for a fresh ashtray and
smoked another cigarette.

Eventually it was done. The last note was tootled and the
trumpet put away in the battered black case. Alan Claire closed
the piano lid and the manager locked it to prevent any more
music escaping.

'You've still got a good lip for the trumpet, Spike,' said Alan.

'And I've got good legs for the trumpet as well,'
replied Spike.

'Yes, if you get them lagged for the winter.'

As we left the restaurant the manager waved us farewell and
collapsed asleep in the arms of a waiter.

I hailed a taxi to wherever I was going and Spike sent
Shelagh to look for their latest blue Mini.

'Yes, I know what colour it is, Spike. But I don't know
where you parked it. You should have drawn a map!'

I adore Shelagh. She has a conspiratorial throaty laugh, her
own sort of war humour for she has had to survive the various
emotional storms that came with the territory – life with Milligan.
Tonight had been perfect, all the orbs of the Universe in perfect
harmony or as Alan Claire put it:

'Good vibes! Night, night, Spike.'

We were alone.

'Spike, what about Singapore? Wasn't that amazing? We fell
through time, didn't we?'

Before Spike could answer, or would he answer? Shelagh
drove up and beeped the horn. She had rationed herself to only one
glass of wine.

'Get in,' she said. 'Can we give you a lift, John?'

'I've got a taxi waiting, thanks. Goodnight.'

As Spike climbed into the Mini he gripped my arm.

'Who killed Captain Witherspoon?' he said.

They drove off into the night.

Would Spike come back with me to Singapore? It was unfair to ask him to. To expect him to want to make a return visit. We had got out easily enough this time, but going back could be asking for trouble.

I got into the taxi.

'Shepherds Bush,' I said. 'Don't hurry. By the time we get there I might have moved to Mayfair.'

The Milligans lived in a Victorian folly called Monkenhurst on Hadleigh Common, North Finchley. While they were there during their Once Upon A Time There Lived A Milligan, I would visit them, walking up the hill from the tube station. As a favoured guest I was lodged in the tower, an extravagant architectural feature.

The downstairs lavatory had a wooden commode and the bottom of the porcelain bowl was engraved with coloured peacocks. When pulling out a piece of toilet paper, the holder played Rule Britannia. It was like a night at the Proms being in Spike's downstairs toilet and one always emerged in a patriotic fervour.

The tower had a pointed turret and I would come out every morning with a pointed head and sit in the kitchen with Jean, the Scottish housekeeper, while I had my breakfast. She could be described as an old retainer for she had been with the family for years, a bulwork of kindness and caring for the children through the years of divorce and illness.

Now only the lovely Jane, the youngest remained – the others having flown the coop. Jean's nannying days were over, though she still performed less hectic duties.

In Allfarthing Lane where I had lived while the marriage was still intact, an elderly Polish couple lived next door. This Polish woman had been in the Warsaw Uprising 1944, carrying soup through the sewers to the Resistance Fighters. They had a housekeeper, by then an Ancient, that they cared for and nursed. So what did become of old housekeepers? Where do they go?

With Ray Galton it was dogs. Frisky, barky, jumpy house dogs better than any burglar alarm. Good companions. But in their turn they became old and sick with various messes to be cleaned up daily until it became time to be a dead dog and be buried in the garden. Ray's garden was like a dog cemetery. But you couldn't do the same to housekeepers, could you?

The lounge was friendly and spacious and in the evening a log fire blazed merrily so that its flames could reflect in the eyes of the genial master of the house.

'It's all paid for, cash!' explained Spike. 'I told you, John, invest in property. You need a home.'

I did need a home. He was right.

The lounge contained various interesting artifacts.

'This bugle,' said Spike, picking up a pitted instrument, 'was played by a trumpeter who lay dying in the Battle of Spien Kop.'

'What rubbish,' exclaimed Shelagh.

'Prove it,' said Spike. 'I will now show you a tea cup washed up by Prince Charles when he was here. It's still badly stained round the bottom and he's coming back to finish the job when he's got time.'

We wrote in Spike's bedroom, which activity was the overall object of my visit. It had a small annexe in which was placed a desk and a typewriter, and files and money lay scattered about the floor. For our sessions he was usually half-dressed and would leap upon an exercise bike in his longjohns, calling out, 'Read that back, John!'

I would read out the sketch while he pedalled madly on the machine.

'I'm trying to get up a sweat,' he gasped.

'Turn the heating up,' I suggested.

I had brought along an idea about a Wimbledon tennis umpire who at home at the tea table used a high umpire's chair and turned his head from one end of the table to the other during the conversation between his wife and the visiting vicar...

```
Wife: How old was our Muriel when she left home?
Umpire: Fifteen love!
Vicar: My daughter didn't leave home till she was much
older...
Umpire: Thirty love!
```

```
Wife: There's no comparison.
Umpire: Thirty fifteen.
Vicar: Well, my Dora she was a bit retarded.
Umpire: Fault. First service.
Vicar: Eight o'clock, Sunday morning. High Mass.
Wife: Do finish the meat balls, Vicar, before they go off.
Umpire: New balls, please!
```

There was a green and gloomy library in the house. I suppose it was an exquisite place but I never saw anybody in there. It was the sort of room, for no reason at all, people bypassed. Had it been haunted, it would have had a lived in feel about it. But no self-respecting ghost would stay in the library when he could enjoy the company of Spike elsewhere.

Back in the lounge, Spike picked up a polished tin that had a dented lid.

'My father had this lucky tobacco tin in his tunic pocket over his heart, when my mother shot him. Terrance, my boy, he would say, smoking saved my life. Even if it does get in the curtains.'

One evening when I was on an over-nighter at Monkenhurst, Barry Humphries and his wife, Diana, came to dinner. Candles were lit in the dining room and the best crockery was produced. It was a sumptuous occasion, atmospheric, like being in the first class salon on the *Titanic* – and the evening, though starting well, duly sank after ice was produced to cool the Chablis.

Barry and Diana were soon to separate so my cheerful remark, 'Don't let an unhappy marriage spoil a perfectly good divorce' pressed all the wrong buttons.

When the crockery had stopped rattling and we were on to coffee and petits fours, Spike suggested that we might like to hear the music to his unproduced masterpiece, *Joseph, I'm Having A Baby*. We all agreed it was a splendid idea and Shelagh disappeared behind a discreet silk screen where the music centre was apparently housed. She returned, smiling, as the first notes wafted over us. It was jolly nice and after about five minutes wrapt listening I started a conversation, assuming it to be pleasant background music.

'Turn it off, Shelagh!' shouted Spike. 'They're not interested! They'd rather talk!'

'It's my fault, Spike,' I said.

'No, it's not your fault,' he replied. 'You were born like that.'

Shelagh went behind the screen and switched the music off. Silence.

'If you ask me, you got a winner there, Spike,' ventured Barry. 'I want to know what happens next.'

'Really? If you've got a bible at home, Barry, you can find out.'

'There's one on the bedside cabinet,' declared Barry. He stood up.

'Well, Diana, my dear, we don't want to keep these good people out of bed. It's nearly half past ten.'

'You can't go this early,' said Spike. 'I haven't insulted everybody yet. Don't spoil my evening.'

Everybody laughed. We climbed out of the lifeboats and the ship sailed on.

I'm in a canal, in a wet suit, dictating a letter...

'Dear Sir, I would be very interested to receive by return of post your most interesting pamphlet *The Release from the Clutch of the Drowning*, as I am currently drowning, Yours sincerely, Jack Tree.'

I disappear under the murky water.

CUT TO Spike and Marty Feldman, postmen in an open boat, rowing toward the spot I disappeared.

Spike takes an envelope from his sack and looks over the side of the boat, scanning the depths. My hand shoots out of the water and takes the envelope and submerges again.

Letter delivered, Spike and Marty row away.

Just another mad afternoon's filming on The Marty Feldman Comedy Machine.

That was in 1972. Labelling a fragment from the broken Time Machine... Put it together again. Punch the ME AND SPIKE button and see where we go. It does not move. OK, I get out and look around. Still in 1972 according to the dial.

That was the year I met Marty Feldman coming out of a football match at Stamford Bridge, Chelsea at home. Sheer chance.

'Hi, John!' Marty's eyes rolled in several directions. 'This is Larry Gelbart. He's script editing my show for ITV, *The Comedy Machine*. Are you available to write for it?'

I was always writing a new play or painstakingly revising *The Looney's* year after year, feeding in my own experiences of a dysfunctional but fun family, and YES I was available.

'Spike's writing for us and he's in it too.'

'OK, Marty. Count me in.'

Which was how I came to be in that canal in quite cold weather, surviving in a wet suit because I liked acting and guess what? Nobody else wanted to do that part. I could have written more drowning parts and made a career for myself in Goon Comedy. It's easy to be wise after the event.

Filming again. My sketch, *The Phantom Trouser Snatcher*. A Victorian melodrama in which men wore their trousers round their ankles because braces and belts had not yet been invented. In the library of Lord Crappington, Home Secretary (Marty), is in conference with Inspector Longwhistler of the Yard (Spike). They pace up and down the room, their trousers round their ankles discussing the latest trouser thefts.

```
'If only we could come up with something to make it harder,
Longwhistler, for this devil and his trouser robberies.'
        'As soon as you sit down, you are at risk. He's in
with his hook...'
        'I've got it! Say that trousers were worn up round
the thighs, to the waist even - and attached in some form
- they'd be almost imposible to remove. Without help, that
is.'
        Spike ponders this.
        'No, my Lordship, a gentleman could not be seen with
his trousers up. He'd be a laughing stock. And he'd be able
to move at four miles an hour. I don't think the human frame
could stand it.'
```

Marty tries very hard not to laugh. He is shaking and his moustache nearly drops off.

'We could say, Longwhistler, that trousers are being worn high this season.'

'True. Perhaps to the knees, Lord Crappington – society might tolerate that - with the long pair of braces. I'd be willing to go that far.'

Then there was the *Beard Straining Contest* (a sketch that came to me in the night) whereby men in leotards with various appliances for straining achieved instant beard growth – and competed with each other.

Marty/Commentator:...And Spike Milligan who last year in the Orpington All-Comers Finals produced a perfect goatee beard that won him two nines, one for thickness texture, and one for grooming, is this evening going for the full King Edward...

SPIKE paces up and down, flexing his muscles, breathing deeply and doing crouches and strange leaps.

Marty/Commentator: Milligan is obviously quite nervous. This is the first time in competition that he has attempted this kind of beard. The King Edward is a definite step up in category, not to be attempted lightly, eh, Hugh?

Hugh: No, definitely not. You may remember that Cecil Wilson ruptured himself last February attempting a King Edward in the Hastings semi-finals, and his wife divorced him and married a sex maniac.

Marty/Commentator: That just goes to show, yes. Now here he goes - Milligan - to the straining bar. I must say he looks quietly confident. Deep breaths. Utter concentration. Silence. And...

SPIKE tenses himself on the bar, then with a grunt contorts himself. A King Edward beard appears on his upper chest.

Marty/Commentator: Oh, God. He's let it slip! It's on his chest. He's disqualified. He's out of the contest. Hard luck, Milligan...

>   A bell rings. A referee steps forward, producing a
> card, and points to the exit. SPIKE gestures theatrically,
> arguing, then leaves in tears.

These sketches for Marty Feldman's *Comedy Machine* and forwards, backwards and sideways for *Milligan in Summer/Autumn*, *Milligan For All Seasons* and various contributions to the *Q* series for the BBC, and *The Last Laugh Before TV AM*, Channel 4... produced endless ideas from me and coming and going to Spike's office and house... and my *Time Machine* (not to be confused with Marty's *Comedy Machine*) dumps me in various places with wonky dials and I step out into the landscape looking for clues.

I am cast back upon the moods of Spike and where they took us. I'm running out of restaurants and conversations desert me and I look for Spike in the most unlikely places...

'Where are you, Milligan? Shall I compare Thee to a summer's day?'

'In ever-damp Neasden, yes. Where they sell umbrellas with shower attachments.'

'Let's go back to Singapore.'

'Damn you, Antrobus. You left me in the lurch there. Arrested by the Red Caps on suspicion of murder by death of Captain I Owe Coutts Thirteen Pounds Ten Witherspoon.'

I could not argue with The Milligan. Next time getting out – back Through The Looking Glass – might not be so easy.

'We don't have to go there, Spike. We can talk about it.'

'That's how it happened last time, John.'

'Are you scared?'

'Bloody right, I am.'

I tricked him in the end. I asked, 'What is the subject, Spike, that you would least like to write for the stage?' and he said, 'The Fall of Singapore, 1942, and the smell of the docks, the burning rubber and the reek of defeat!'

And we were there...

The blood orange sun was perched on the horizon about to launch into an orbit that we call a day. A day when more people would die ridiculously in Singapore and only a few with sighs of contentment for a life well lived, surrounded by a devoted family and a fringe of sightseers peering through a beaded curtain into a shadowed room hazed with incense.

I accelerated, getting the last ounce of speed from the sedate family Hudson Saloon that Spike and I had commandeered at gun point. Milligan was in the custody of the Red Caps now, as far as I was concerned, and it was up to me to rescue the Ragtag platoon from the impending Friendly Fire bombardment on the Royal Singapore Golf Links.

Seeing no gate to the right I pulled the wheel over and lurched off the road, shattering the light wooden boundary fence, bouncing on to the lush turf of a putting green. The car stalled. I leapt out and found the starting handle in the boot before hurrying forward to crank start the wretched machine.

'You need a bit more choke, mate.'

I looked up to see Dickens leaning over the bonnet, an unlit dog-end in the corner of his mouth.

'I don't want to flood the carburettor.'

'Don't worry. I used to work in a garage.'

Dickens tickled the choke while I cranked the engine. It coughed and came to life, just like Dickens did every morning.

'Hop in,' he said, occupying the driver's seat. 'Where do you want to go, mate? Back on the road?'

I jumped in beside him, slamming the door.

'The Ninth Hole, Eric. The CO's arranged a bombardment. Dawn plus 12, to teach Captain Thomas a lesson.'

Dickens glanced at his watch.

'Christ! That gives us about two minutes. Hang on...'

Dickens put his foot down and sped across the turf. All I could see were various white poles sticking up on the skyline and no sign of the Ragtags.

'Which is it? Are they there?'

'Aye, they're still kippo. '

'We've got to get off the links on time, Dickens!'

'Don't worry, I've got errant bridegrooms to the altar. Pregnant mothers to the hospital. All on time. You haven't got a train to catch, have you? Don't worry.'

I saw a figure bobbing up out of a dip. It was Captain Thomas, Retarded. He started waving his stick at the car and running towards us. Eric put his palm on the hooter and left it there. Heads stuck up in front of us on a green. It was the Ragtag platoon.

Eric skidded to a halt, churning up the giddy grass. He nonchalantly called through the window,

'Jump in, lads. Chop chop! The Artillery's dropping a barrage on our positions.'

'When?' asked Alan, yawning.

'Oh, in about thirty seconds.'

They crammed into the car, grabbing whatever equipment came to hand and abandoning the rest. As Captain Thomas laboured on to the green, for some foolish reason I climbed out of the car and saluted him.

'Oh, Christ,' he gasped, staring at the deep ruts in his beloved turf. 'What devil possessed you to do this? I'll have you all court-martialled and shot.'

'Get into the car, sir. Please! I've no time to explain...'

'Explain? Explanations will get you nowhere, you Devil's Spawn!'

He began beating me with his stick. Eric honked the horn, leaning out of the window.

'Any more for the joyride? Come on, John. The Royal Artillery are known for their promptness.'

I made one last lunge to grab Thomas's arm but he beat me off with the knobbly walking stick, cursing me. I fell into the back of the car as Eric reversed off the links, leaving the mad Welshman, tears streaming down his face, collapsed on the green, seeking to stuff turf back into the deep ruts.

'We can't leave him there!'

'Why not?' said Eric. 'The world could do with one less twit round here.'

Hardly had he spoken than the first shell fell, exploding about fifty yards from the Ninth Hole. The second one burst not far from the Hudson, rocking it on its springs. Private Dixon, ex-taxi driver, seemed to know where the next shell would fall for, twisting and turning, skidding and bucking the bronco Hudson, he got us off the links.

I looked back. Smoke. Explosions. Flying turf. No sign of Captain Thomas except, unless it was my imagination playing tricks, I saw a walking stick tossed spinning in the air. Dirt falling back to earth, the Ninth Hole a cratered grave to its crazed caretaker.

We were stopped at the roadblock and would have stopped anyway to make enquiries about our mukka, Bombardier Milligan. We hoped the MPs had not beaten the crap out of him.

The broken-nosed Lieutenant with the high-pitched voice was surprisingly non-violent, if not pleasant, when he saw us.

'I've got further orders for you squaddies,' he announced. 'From Colonel Harrington. You're to report to him at The Raffles Hotel.'

'Where's Bombardier Milligan?' I demanded.

'We sorted that one out. He was bomb-happy, wouldn't, you know.'

'I know, sir.'

'You should have told us.'

'I tried…'

'That it was Captain Witherspoon all the time. He was in a state of shock alright. Turns out it was this bloke Milligan that was murdered.'

'No, sir, you've got the wrong end of the stick there.'

'Don't tell me which end of the stick I'm holding, soldier. Be on your way.'

Had Milligan changed tack and convinced them he was Captain Witherspoon? Or had orders come from Regimental HQ to that effect?

I returned to the car and climbed in the front seat.

'To The Raffles Hotel,' I ordered Dickens.

We would soon find out…

I woke up in a sweat. I was in bed and the early morning light filtered through the window curtains. I was on the 19th floor of a tower block in North Westminster, nowhere near Big Ben. I was scared to go stand by the windows and enjoy the view because I felt drawn into the void between sky and earth, clouds and tarmac, eternity and traffic. The noise of a city awakening surprisingly carried to the flat. I lay there awhile, adjusting to the fact that the streets below were not Singapore City, not the Bukit Timah Road teeming with deserters and refugees, but commuter cars and delivery lorries on the Harrow Road. And maybe among them a blue Mini, rattling with money, and with The Milligan on the way to his office.

I turned up later at 9 Orme Court, bearing a paper bag containing six jam doughnuts. As usual I poked my head round the door and said hello to Norma Farnes, Spike's agent.

Norma said, 'He's upstairs, John. Is he expecting you?'

'God knows what he's expecting, Norma. Except death and taxes.'

Norma laughed.

'Spike seems quite happy today. It's unnerving. There's only one way he can go, isn't there?'

'Down.'

'Right. Especially when he's so bright early in the day. Something's bound to upset him along the way, then he'll like as not blame me.'

'Don't take it personally,' I said. 'Detach with love, Norma.'

'He can find ways to make me wrong that I wouldn't have dreamt of in a thousand years,' she sighed, and we laughed again.

'The last thing Spike's going to say is that he needs you,' I told her.

Norma and I were good friends and she would relate with her dour Yorkshire humour the latest absurd Milligan story like when his world collapsed because a prop nose was three inches too short though it was exactly the same nose as before – or something else that bothered him. I had as much fun with Norma some days as I did with Spike.

It's a cliché that a successful man needs a good woman behind him. Spike Milligan needed two women and was lucky to find them, Norma Farnes, his enduring agent, and his third wife, Shelagh. I do not know what else they had in common but one thing they did share – a great sense of humour.

I went to have a word with Janet, the attractive receptionist. She had taken the job as a temp, months – or was it years? – ago, and stayed. Such is life. Indeed Shelagh Milligan had also arrived at Orme Court to do a day's temping.

Spike had dictated about forty letters to Shelagh, putting the world to rights – one to the Pope threatening to resign as a Catholic if he did not support a ban on animal experiments – and she had typed them up and taken them back upstairs to him, apprehensive that The Great Man would find fault, but he did not.

Downstairs again, Shelagh was about to leave when Norma said, 'Spike rang down and asked if you're still here. He wants to see you.'

Shelagh once more climbed the stairs. Had he spotted a spelling error?

'Come in, Shelagh. Would you like to have dinner tonight?'

'Yes.'

Proving that there can be nothing so permanent as temping. When Norma Farnes arrived the first day to work for Spike, Ray Galton told her, 'You won't last two weeks with him.'

How wrong can you get?

Perhaps there was something in Spike – I am sure there was a constancy of heart, despite his sometimes awful behaviour.

When Spike was chilled out on his second jam doughnut, I said,

'We were in Singapore again, weren't we?'

Spike considered this. He knew I had not been drinking, that I had put the bottle down and that was that, but some brain cells had obviously been destroyed during the years of carousing and were there enough left to make the right connections? Or to put it bluntly, were there a few light bulbs missing on the Albert Bridge?

'I haven't been back to Singapore, John.'

'So you admit you were there?'

'Did you see me there?'

'Not last time. No, because I had to get our platoon off the golf links. So… what? I mean, Spike, did you convince the Military Police that you were Captain Witherspoon?'

Spike locked the door.

'Look, John, between ourselves – we don't want to go back to the Fall of Singapore. It gets worse, believe me. It's a disaster. Not to be caught up in. I've been through one campaign with the

8th Army in North Africa. Then Italy. Look, I'm already bomb-happy, John…'

'But we're only going Through The Looking Glass, Spike.'

'We might have already done that to get here. This could be Through The Looking Glass Land.'

'Then how do we get back?'

'To where? If Alice had married and had children with the Mad Hatter, she wouldn't want to get back.'

Spike was not going to cooperate. This time round. I did not want to go back to Our War on my own. I would have to think of another way to get out of the Westminster Council tower block.

I was in Cambridge, directing a musical version of my play, *Jonah*. Spike phoned and asked if I would come to London and write a TV series with him because he had fallen out with another writer who was going to help.

I was in love with the leading actress and refused though she said go. After all the play was open. The work was done. But I stalled and said to Spike that I would be back in a week or two.

By the time I got back to London the opportunity had gone. The actress soon abandoned me. I was still in the tower block, divorcing, the three children living with me. My hold on reality was not so hot. I imagined that through a lot of affirmations, affirmative prayer, I would prosper and get out of a council flat into property more befitting my station in life.

I decreed this was to be by a resurgence of a theatrical career. Cameron Mackintosh had come to see the production in Cambridge, said 'no thanks' and left.

I had not considered that my prayers may have been best answered by being of help to someone else, in this case Spike Milligan. I wanted to prove that I needed no-one, but we are all inter-dependent rather than co-dependent. I wanted to be INDEPENDENT, so why bother with the rest of the human race? Except as supporting cast for my own ambitions.

Some people we are called to be with in natural affinity. There's no shame in needing each other, though Life will always find another way, another channel, if one clogs up – in this case me.

Perhaps I have learnt enough to realise that it was not just Spike. It was not him becoming crochety or adopting a role of Neglected Genius. It was me who said 'no' on several occasions, trying to protect myself. From what? Well, I imagined there were two sorts of writing – scriptwriting that you did until you had enough money to pursue the major work of playwrighting or really EGO building.

I was still trying to fix myself, not with drink, alcohol, but with glitter and glitz, fame and fortune. It came and went. It was never enough. And it never did the trick. It never fixed me.

And thus my friendships suffered. This one with Spike Milligan, that I laud and praise, I slowly starved. It's alright to talk about Spike and his terrible defects of character and to tell the tales of his legendry rudeness, to myself included, but I was there too in the mix. And that small refusal to work with Spike, hardly part of the Big Picture, tells as much about our relationship as any other incident.

However, if you allowed that nobody could work together fruitfully upon this planet unless they were perfect, precious little would get done. I do not believe the best way to work out our personal salvation is on a mountain top but rather at the pit-face of human relationships.

Despite our growing apart, Spike and I had more fireworks to produce. The show was still spasmodically on the road.

Chantry Point. One of two asbestos towers, courtesy of the Westminster Council, where I was housed with the three kids, now teenagers. They were available to visit Maggie (my soon to be ex) or stay with her, but in the parting of the ways this is how things had panned out.

In this magic tower I waited for the call. Fame and fortune were hovering. I never gave up. Apart from writing the occasional sketch with Spike, I had been thriving on the fringe with a season of my plays at the Gate Theatre, Notting Hill. Lou Stein, artistic director, directed *Hitler In Liverpool* (in which I played Alois, Hitler's older brother, the black sheep of the family) and also *Up In The Hide*.

I directed *One Orange for the Baby*. There was a flurry of interest, not much money and John Calder (the ever courageous publisher) put them into a volume, *Hitler In Liverpool*.

So, what next? Only the BBC Radio critics had signalled the importance of *One Orange for the Baby*, but this did not wake up the world. I was sinking back into obscurity. Not that I was particularly unhappy. I continued in sobriety and love affairs came and went.

Nicky, Lou and Danny (my kids) were good companions, making sense of life as best they could. Lou acquired a puppy, promising to train it, but like most teenagers she was mysteriously busy and it was left to me. Getting the dog used to doing its toilet outside meant going down nineteen floors and back a dozen times a day, using the metal box lift for tinned people when it was working. I don't know why I chose this method but it passed the time and a writer will look for any excuse to avoid the empty page.

Since getting sober I have always been keen on 'self-help' books like *The Power of Your Subconscious*, Joseph Murphy, *The Game of Life and How to Play It*, Florence Scovell Shin, and many versions and varieties of books like *Your Millionaire Mind* (or is that a book I am going to write?).

I considered that being a writer, I was otherwise unemployable and regarded myself as rich and that every day's awakening left me free to pen another tale. Not always money-rich, to be sure, but never doing a job to get by. I was not tempted and regarded such 'would be' temporary expedients as dangerous. Just For Today I would remain resolutely A WRITER. I have been the despair of many sensible Grown Up People, but I have seen what being realistic has done for them – all very depressing. Looming around, being responsible and polishing their furniture. Speaking in deep voices so that they don't frighten the horses. Planning their retirement and even prepared to meet 'those final expenses', i.e. their own funeral, with the glib satisfaction that they have stayed the financial course. 'Those final expenses!' The last hurdle cleared. Well done. Missing a One Off Golden Opportunity to die millions of pounds in debt.

Anyway in Asbestos Towers I lived with my family and my ideas, and my prayers and affirmations, and 'Lo and behold' one afternoon in January 1981, the phone did ring and it was Peter Sellers.

I had already sent and received a Christmas card from him so the portents were there.

He was phoning from Paris (where I now sit and write, Chantry Point having been pulled down years ago. Thank God I had grown my hair and climbed down the outside of the building and escaped).

Peter was filming *The Fiendish Plot of Doctor Fu Manchu* in the Studio de Boulogne for Orion Films. He explained that the most recent director had departed, filming had stopped and they needed a writer (me!) to sort out the script quickly. Could I come to Paris that very afternoon?

'Tomorrow.' I said, as I had a date that evening, so they all stood round in Paris, cast and crew and Orion Executives, waiting for this unknown entity, John Antrobus, whom Sellers had insisted would cure all, to arrive.

The next morning I descended the nineteen floors in the urine fragrance of the lift and made my way to Heathrow, thence First Class to Paris, to the Lancaster Hotel, just off the Champs Elysées.

I was shown into a luxurious Louis the Something or Other suite and reflected that I would probably not be back in time to collect my Social Security benefit next Thursday. In fact there was a likelihood that I would not be able to sign on again for some time. It was scary.

When I arrived I was wearing a beard and a combat jacket and had a street cred, a sort of pavement energy (that you get from queuing for London buses in all weathers) that inspired respect. One Orion Executive asked me if I was the new director. It would only have taken a 'yes' from me to get the job. Everything was up for grabs and millions of dollars were at stake here.

One of the first people to greet me at the hotel was the charming and ever-helpful Sue, Sellers' secretary and PA. She thrust a drink into one hand and the script into another and asked me if I needed anything else. I had a list of Life Goals but made do with a saucer of peanuts to be going on with.

David Tomlinson paid me great attention. As the writer of new scenes I had a limited shelf life, I suppose. For at the Press showing of the film in Leicester Square some months later he quite ignored me. John Le Mesurier was vague and affable, much as you would expect to find him in any episode of *Dad's Army*. Helen Mirren said hello and that was that.

I was still seated in the lounge when Peter arrived and gave me a big hug and asked me if I thought filming could resume on Tuesday, it then being Sunday evening.

'I don't see why not,' I replied, diplomatically, not having a clue.

'Good! I knew you'd sort it out, Johnny! Have you read the script yet?'

The script was in a brown envelope in front of me on the coffee table.

'Not yet, Peter.'

'Don't let it put you off! Do what you like with it! Only hurry up because everybody's on full pay.' Peter burst out laughing. He seemed supremely confident that I was the man for the job.

That night I read the script. It was the least I could do. There was plenty to like about the writing but the story, possibly after many rewrites, was confusing, lacking motive. I made some notes. First impressions. Do-able.

Keep It Simple. Where had I read that?

The next morning I was whisked to the studios to see the rushes of what had already been filmed. It was hoped that any revisions would include this work, so far accomplished. Then we had a script conference…

Everybody held their breath because basically was I going to come up with the goodies? Or catch the next plane home? Economy class. With nothing but expenses.

I must say I was blithely confident. It was the sort of job I could do, for way back in my army days at Sandhurst I had been taught to be lucid. To make a tactical appraisal and come up with a course of action. The War Office never got full credit, until now, for helping to rescue *The Fiendish Plot of Doctor Fu Manchu*.

Everybody liked my ideas which put the story on its feet and carried the scenes to a happy conclusion, including all the ones that had already been shot. The art was to recognise the value of what was there in the script and to underpin it, and clarify.

I was given the best office and asked how much money I wanted for the job. I under-priced myself by a factor of ten. I've never heard people say 'yes' so quickly. After all my Self-Help book training I had forgotten the first principle – let them make the first offer. It could be way beyond what you had in mind.

Filming re-commenced the next day. Peter Sellers took over as director and as no-one thought he would conspire to fire himself – he had gone through five directors – a measure of stability was restored. Because I had laid out the plot line they could continue to shoot scenes already in the script, with minor amendments and deletions, while I wrote the new scenes.

I would take my hot-off-the-typewriter pages along to Peter in his dressing room. Often he would be laid out upon his couch, an oxygen mask clutched to his face.

Sellers by then could be described as, 'not a well man'. Playing the part of 120-year-old Fu Manchu desperately seeking the elixir of life did not require much make-up. Peter himself could have done with such a potion. Like Fu Manchu, who had only months to live unless he found a remedy, the clock was ticking for Peter as well. It was uncanny.

Sellers also played the part of the Inspector called out of retirement to apprehend his arch-enemy Fu Manchu.

'I am yin to his yang,' the Inspector pondered his inscrutable foe.

I would have liked more room, a cleaner page, to have developed the Fu Manchu/Inspector relationship, but it was not practical. I would read out my latest scene and invariably Peter would say something like, 'Right, Johnny, get it printed up. Let's see if we can get Alfie Bass for the Ceremony of the Keys scene at the Tower Of London.'

'Who knocks upon the door?'

'The holder of the King's keys.'

'Enter Kinky Holder.'

'Ere, do you mind…?'

Or something like that. A far cry, perhaps, from my aspirations to be a major playwright and SPEAK FOR ENGLAND. But then I did work on the first Carry On film.

I wrote a key scene (not the kinky scene) which was the birthday celebration of Fu Manchu – when he is to drink the elixir of life, this rare and vital fluid. But such is the blazing forest of candles upon his birthday cake that they set fire to the clothing of the monk carrying the elixir and he drops it. Thus starting the panic to obtain the ingredients of another dose which include the ground-down powder of the Crown Jewels of England.

'Good,' said Peter. 'We'll get Bert Quock over to play the monk.'

Bert appeared a few days later and we filmed the scene. He did not have to act alarm as his prop jacket caught fire. It was getting out of control as he dropped the glass phial and beat the flames desperately.

'Cut!'

Prop men rushed forward with a blanket and put Bert out.

'Very good, Bert,' chuckled Peter. 'Now we'll do your close up.'

Bert's eyes widened.

'Close up? No close up, thank you very much! I don't need close up, Peter!'

But he endured another take, being the pro he is.

It's funny, you write a scene out of your mind and a few days later Bert Quock is standing in front of the cameras, his jacket on fire. Mind you, he has not spoken to me since.

During filming news came that my father had died. Peter could not have been more solicitous. He was the first person with whom I shared the news, going to his hotel room at seven in the morning. He gave me a big hug and made sure that my trip back to Cumbria for the funeral was arranged, First Class return with a car from Manchester Airport.

To gain the approval of one's father is ever an oldest son's quest. It was reported to me that in hospital Dad had said to the nurses, 'My son, John, is working in Paris with Peter Sellers.'

Not exactly his last words, as I would have preferred, but pretty close.

The next day I was back in Paris, flashing past the Christmas lights of the Champs Elysées in the chauffeured limousine towards Studio de Boulogne. I tried not to think about Cumbria, Drigg, and the sadness of recent days. Dad was gone and with his emphysema, hardly surprising. Rakish, raffish smoking days long gone, but he had started at age fourteen and not stopped till he was fifty. By then the damage was done.

Lynne Frederick, Sellers' wife, arrived in Paris, her role being to support her husband, though why she needed my office to do this, I don't know. She needed a door to put her name on, that's for sure, with the title Executive Producer. She had the 'street smarts' to look after her own interests, something I obviously lacked. This is not a criticism. Look and learn. I liked her, even though I was moved to a much smaller office. But don't complain. They took the vacuum cleaner out.

One evening Sellers took Lynne, Sue and myself to a restaurant. It was a low-key evening, but not depressing… until Peter excused himself from the table when coffee was being served – with a weak smile – and we all assumed he was going to the toilet. However, that was the last we saw of him.

Sue looked outside the restaurant and Bert, the driver, and the car were missing. She came back to report. Peter had obviously returned to the hotel.

'He's done it again!' exclaimed Lynne, bursting into tears.

Marty Baum, Peter Sellers' agent, turned up from California and he told me that I would be invited to write the next *Pink Panther* script. My spirits were high, for I was out of the woods, a Hollywood scriptwriter in my own mind. My job was done. I packed my bags. No point in hanging around, I decided. I did not notice the possibility of assisting Peter with the direction and I was missing my kids and life on the fringe. Theatre. I had my dreams intact. I needed to dream them for a little while longer, rather than live them. I needed to prepare for a new life in California.

However, a few months later Peter Sellers died of a heart attack in the Middlesex Hospital, London, and my dreams temporarily died with him.

A footnote. While we were in Paris a copy of *Being There* was sent over from California and Peter arranged a private showing. I laughed like a drain throughout, and was the only one that did so. Several people scolded me afterwards. Only I had seen it as a comic masterpiece and I assured Peter that it was just that, wonderfully funny, for even he did not seem to know.

It was this Hal Ashby directed film that set the seal of genius upon the life work of Peter Sellers.

Back to Spike…

PART V

ADVENTURES IN A TIME MACHINE

'And what is the name of reality?' asked Hairy.
'I don't know,' said Wallop. 'Except that I
guess it's something to be experienced.'
He paused.
'And experience is something to be avoided.
It leads to too many anecdotes…'

The Nature of Inertia
John Antrobus

Mate (Chris Langham): Well, this 'ere's a waiting room, mate... so are you waiting for a train to come in... or are you waiting to go on one?
Spike: No, I'm just waiting... I'm a purist...
Mate: 'Ere, they won't let you use the waiting room just for waiting you know - the station police'll bung you out, mate.
Spike: I expect to be persecuted for my ideas, but one day people will come to waiting rooms and they'll just wait - you'll see. Then you won't need trains... not to come and go... that will all seem very old-fashioned soon.
Mate: What you mean all the stations..? They'll just be...
Spike: Just be waiting rooms... King's Cross, Euston, Croinge, people will just go there and wait...
Mate: What wait to die?
Spike: No, that would be cheating.
Mate: No, but if they waited long enough they would die.
Spike: Yes, but that's one of the hazards of the waiting profession.
Mate: But what about the people who came in here waiting for trains?
Spike: What, the traditionalists? Well, we would reason with them and if that didn't work...
Mate: Yes.
Spike: We'd hit 'em.
Mate: Well, how would you know the ones to hit, mate?
Spike: Pardon?
Mate: How can you tell the difference between the ones waiting for the trains and the ones waiting to wait?
Spike: Yes, it's better to hit the lot of them. That way no-one feels left out.
Mate: It's going to be a new world, isn't it?
Spike: Yes, beautiful to behold - massage parlours every-where - and jelly-wobbling competitions for kids.
Mate: How do you wobble a jelly, mate?
Spike: The best way to wobble a jelly, mate, is to go to a place that has a lot of earthquakes. And wait.
Mate: Wait? Wait? What for? Wait for an earthquake, mate?
Spike: No, just wait, mate. Don't forget your calling.

From 'The Incredible Case of the Vanishing Flying Scotsman', *The Milligan Papers.*

Spike Milligan, comedian and writer, was born in Ahmednagar, India, on April 16, 1918. He died in Rye, East Sussex, on February 27, 2002, aged 83.

The Times, 28 February 2002

It is raining in Paris. I am not writing but rather watching the telly – World Cup, June 2002, in Ibaraki, South Korea.

Ireland are trailing Germany 1–0…

And I'm thinking Spike would have liked to watch this match and say funny things about the Irish players like,

'They look worried. They don't know where they're staying tonight.'

We are into 3 minutes' time added on and every foray at the German goal has led to disappointment, SO FAR, and I say to myself, perhaps Spike can see this somewhere and 'Come on, lads! Do something magical for him, The Milligan!'

My mind whispers, keep looking, or was that Spike? And the next moment Robbie Keane scores. He does not execute a perfect aerial somersault like the USA player earlier today, but a clumsy cartwheel followed by a muddy forward roll (the Irish have brought their own rain), but who cares, the ball is in the back of the net.

'Thanks, Spike.'

'I told you so.'

'Are you now my guardian angel?'

'Well, who do you want? Me or Peter Sellers?'

So the sibling rivalry still goes on.

Peter is sitting on a cloud. It is tobacco smoke due to a recent Royal arrival.

Sellers: It's not worth fighting over, Spike. You can be John Antrobus's guardian angel.

Milligan: I'm too busy organising a demo to preserve St Peter's Gate. The new plan to get into Heaven is through electronic turnstiles using swipe cards.

Sellers: What's wrong with that?

Milligan: Nothing, if you're a Barbarian.

Sellers: You've got to move with the times, Spike. Anyone's allowed up to two guardian angels, you know.

Milligan: Not of my quality, they're not. I've just been inside Robbie Keane's right boot helping him score for Ireland.

How can they refuse me? Peter Sellers and Spike Milligan. I believe in both of them. And it would give Jesus a rest.

Spike (*looking down upon me with great compassion*): You wrote a nice piece about Peter Sellers' death, didn't you?

John: Thank you.

Spike: Except that it was too long. He's not interesting like I am.

John: Sorry.

Spike: What about my obiturary?

John: I haven't got to it yet.

Spike: I died for you, John, to publicise your book. I hope you realise that.

John: Taa, Spike. It couldn't have come at a better time.

Spike: That's what I've always been good at. Timing.

John: Thanks again.

Spike: You could compose a hymn to me, like 'Now thank we all our Spike.'

John: I will. I'll become a devout Milliganist. How can I sum up your life on earth, Spike?

Spike: With a great… (*he blows a raspberry*)

John: Unpredictable, that's what you were. Afraid to be ordinary? Maybe. Did you ever have an ordinary day?

Spike: Never. I left that to Sellers. He was very ordinary except in his talents. Yes, he was a genius as an actor. He had to be to get away from his own nonentity. When he wasn't acting, he had the personality of a Golders Green accountant doing the Yorkshire Ripper's entertainment allowances.

John: Very good. I'll put that in.

Spike: Are you going to my Memorial Service, John?

John: Yes, Spike, I have been invited.

Spike: With all the other crawlers, eh? I'm glad the BBC is organising it, because they made sure I was dead and buried years ago. It's been a long wait for them.

John: The BBC gave you a broadcast 80th birthday party, Spike. To share with the Nation.

Spike: Because Terry Wogan needed the money. They felt guilty about neglecting me. The BBC thought I was dead until someone phoned them up and said he's still breathing, you know.

John: You do underestimate how much you are appreciated.

Spike: Appreciated? I changed the face of English humour and all I get is St Martin's-in-the-Field for my Memorial Service, while Harry Secombe got Westminster Abbey because he could sing 'Onward Christian Soldiers' louder than anyone else. Can you imagine how Winston Churchill felt to have shared the Abbey with a man famous for his shaving routine in Coventry? It's all crap. Are they going to put up a statue of Secombe in Whitehall holding a shaving brush and mug? And then paint him pink and say he was gay?

John: I'm writing all this down.

Spike: Good. Write what you like. I'm dead. I can't sue. Tell them what a bastard I was.

John: We all have our off days, Spike.

Spike: Being a bastard was a good day.

Spike was being unfair on Harry Secombe and Peter Sellers. But then insults were his stock in trade. He would compose an insult and wait for the right opportunity to use it. Most of it was quite indiscriminate. It was whoever happened to come along, the same way the Vietcong would lay landmines.

I've lost Spike. I don't know where to find him. He's breaking up on me. I can't hear him. I go and stand in the street. No, he's gone…

I find myself with two options. The first is to enter my Time Machine, but it's wonky. I pull all sorts of levers and dials spin, steam escapes and a mechanical voice says, 'Abbey Road. George Martin. Milligan Preserved.'

That sounds interesting so I press a green button and wait for a whirry, clunky sound like a cuckoo clock gathering itself to pounce... and when it stops, I open the door and find myself parked on a zebra crossing, no sign of The Beatles.

I join Spike going into the foyer of the recording studios.

'Where have you been, John?'

'I came here by Time Machine, Spike.'

'What was the traffic like?'

'Congested around the year 2000. I had trouble getting through.'

George Martin appears and greets us.

'Hello, Spike! Hello, John!'

'Hello, George...'

'How are you today, Spike?'

'I'm not a psychiatrist. How would I know?'

'His mother used to cuff him round the head when he was a child,' I say. 'So he's ambivalent about women.'

'OK,' says George, beaming. 'This way, folks.'

He takes us through to a recording studio.

'I'm going to be behind that glass screen,' says George.

'In case we catch tuberculosis,' says Spike.

'You just press this switch if you want to talk to me in the control booth, right?'

'Not much likelihood of that,' says Spike.

'He's communicating in the only way he knows how,' I explain.

'I understand,' says George. 'Don't worry. I have a rich relationship with Spike. This is one of his good days...'

Spike suddenly stirs from his torpor.

'How about a cup of tea, George?' he suggests.

'I thought you'd never ask, Spike.'

Tea is produced. And biscuits for a sugar rush and soon we are all chatting away merrily. The clouds have dispersed from The Milligan psyche and we are set fair to record 'The Hit Parade' for Spike's record which also contains the 'Ying Pong Tiddle I Po' song.

Afterwards Spike says cheerily, pleased with our morning's work, quickly done after all, 'Can I give you a lift, John?'

'No thanks. Bye bye.'

I return to my Time Contrivance which is surrounded by a curious crowd, including a couple of Bluebottles. I push my way past and enter the machine, closing the door and pulling a few random levers before anyone objects. Ah, yes PRESS THE GREEN BUTTON... JOB DONE...

The whirring noise. A couple of clunks. A voice announces as though I were in a lift at Harrods,

'Broadcasting House. Recording of *The Dinosaurs*, 1977.'

Oh, we get a date this time, do we?

I meet Spike in the studio to record with him my two-hander play. John Scotney is directing and of course he says, 'How are you today, Spike?'

'He doesn't know. He's not a psychiatrist,' I answer quickly. 'His mother used to hit him.'

Spike laughs. 'How about a cup of tea, John?'

Scotney has been forewarned.

'And jam doughnuts,' he says.

It's going to be a good day.

Back in my Not A Tardis Thingy. It's a shaky ride this time. Turbulence. Perhaps we are passing through the Paris student riots, 1968. I have no way of knowing. It settles down and I guess we have landed. The voice says, 'Lingerie department.'

I step out and find The Milligan buying expensive lingerie. We are in Harrods.

'Who's it for?' I ask him.

'The wife. It's a reconciliation present. I want her to forgive me for working 18 hours a day these last six weeks to the verge of a nervous breakdown to pay for all her extravagances. I want her to forgive me for not being an idiot who appreciates her friends and their stupid jokes. And to forgive me for being so bloody talented, in fact A GENIUS! But she doesn't seem to understand – It's Not My Fault!'

'I know, Spike,' I say. 'It's something you were born with. You have to live with it.'

'Yes, but I don't know how much longer I can live with her.' He looks at me wildly. 'She's holding my children hostage.'

His eyes are moist. What is it about Harrods that reduces grown men to tears.

I guessed we were way back early years, first marriage, I'd say – and all I wanted was to get home. For the energies were dangerous here.

'I've got to go, Spike. You can't change anybody else, and they can't change you. It's no good getting married saying, "I'll work on him or her later".'

'The biological urge to procreate makes fools of us,' raged Spike. 'Why do you think I'm here?'

The assistant nervously wrapped the peachy silk nightdress that nestled in white tissue paper, tying it with a pretty ribbon and attaching a red seal.

'The mind and body do not belong together. Evolution has blundered – gone up a blind alley – and we will be wiped out like the dinosaurs. The sooner the better.'

'How do you want to pay, sir?'

'With my blood of course.'

Spike produced a Harrods Gold Account card and handed it to the woman.

'Oh, you share this with Mrs Milligan? She's often in here,' said the pert assistant, recovering.

'I know where she comes,' replied Mr Milligan, darkly. He turned to me as the purchase was processed.

'I am at war with myself,' he observed.

Words came into my head.

'My house is rent asunder and must surely fall. That mine enemies may enter therein, and lay waste the pretty courtyards and poison the fountains, and tear down the vines that were tender with fruit. But this year's crop shall make sour vinegar pressed unto my lips...'

'Where's that from?' demanded Milligan.

'Where it all comes from, Spike. The Great Nowhere.'

'Sign here, sir, if you please.'

Spike signed with his usual flourish as if he had just negotiated the Unconditional Surrender of Japan, and picked up his package. There was a note of triumph in his voice as he said, 'Nice bit of lingerie, mate. Always does the trick.' The anger had vanished, spent as a summer storm, and now we had the Lad from Lewisham who had done ever so well. A favoured Gold Card customer. He could buy the store.

Jekyll and Hyde. He often rewrote the story into sketch form and loved to play it, even in his office where he would collapse behind his desk clutching his throat, thrash around on the floor groaning, trying not to giggle, then re-emerge – his face contorted with two plastic joke vampire teeth he had fixed in his mouth. He even went to see his bank manager once and did the vampire teeth routine, collapsing off his chair and then straightening up, demanding a reduction in his overdraft charges.

Milligan's favourite play was Strindberg's *The Father*. He wrote his own version and planned to play the anti-hero, driven mad by his wife and coaxed into a strait-jacket by his old nanny. Van Gogh was not enough some days.

'Farewell, Spike. Good luck with the Biological Urge tonight.'

I returned to the lift area while Spike went his own way to the perfumery department to buy another present for his wife.

I was confronted by six sets of doors. I selected the ones with a light above reading, Going Up, and as the doors opened I entered the lift, after stepping aside for a woman with extremely high heels who was also extremely highly scented.

I pressed a few numbers – actually the sequence of my birth date and waited hopefully…

The lights blinked and went out as the sedately furnished box shook more and more violently. When the lights came on again, I was in my Time Machine hurtling through Don't Look Now doors opening dinosaurs extinct, according to Spike, looking for dinner. Pressing every button in sight the door shut my hand jammed against the panel praying Home James and so it turned out. Exit contraption.

Lesson: Never buy a second-hand Time Machine, especially from Terry Nation, creator of the Darleks who hate stairs and love chasing endlessly down well-polished corridors giving orders in strangled tin tones like DON'T SCRATCH THE LINO!

I am back to The Ever Unfolding Blissful Moment.

Now.

It may be peaceful but it's active and pushes me on,' Don't rest your arse on God's doorstep, chum. We have work to do.'

OK, Option Two. Singapore. I might find Spike there. But that strata of time does not lend itself to easy access and a clanking contrivance of steam valves, rods and bolts, oil drips, and blurred images on cracked screens, won't take me there. It's kaput. Wait…

Fragments of Spike. The broken mirror. There is the Universal Spike, The Good Soldier Spike, The Lover, The Statesman, The Hero, The Coward, The Comedian, The Author… I cannot imagine an end to Spike. A point of LIGHT that produces form, a body… that lives, sickens and dies, but not the LIGHT… It is focused, essence of Spike and the star from which he burst may have died but He Is The Light and must travel for eternity, making forms of himself, entering worlds, charged with energy. Making trouble. Making love and laughter. Moving on…

So I wait. Quietly. The book must end. Surely. But not the life of Spike Milligan. I cannot come to the end of that. Speaking personally. I am always on the threshold of another day with him, pristine, full of promise, beautiful hours…

I go to the mirror and shout, 'SINGAPORE!'

And nothing happens.

I sit in tears for want of him. One moment I allow myself. Of grief. Of separation. It cannot be… I would rent my clothes were they not already in rags, the latest fashion.

I must wait. Till I hear the sound of the guns. Distant at first. Coming closer. I smell the rubber burning, burning in the go-downs. I hear the shriek of a diving Zero and flinch… and pull the steering wheel, left, LEFT, instinctively, and I am off the road – foot jammed on the brake pedal, skidding to a halt in the Hudson family saloon and my family-sized Ragtag platoon grit their teeth. Duck. The explosion, explosion, explosions, a string of bombs fall quite far off. Silence.

'Your bloody driving's more dangerous than the Japs, mate,' mutters Dickens.

'Give him back the wheel, for Christ's sake,' says Ferguson, nursing a bruised lip he has just banged on the Bren Gun.

Roy smiles like a Botticelli angel and says, illustrating that beauty and banality often live together, 'Dickens knows his way round Redcar.'

'Harrogate,' corrects Dickens. 'I used to drive parties from Harrogate to the Redcar races. Now that was a good day out.'

'You drive, Dickens,' I order the scummy busted-twice sergeant, a trouble-maker if I ever I saw one, but a man who could get you out of a tight spot as well.

'Well, make up your mind,' he says, insolently, but what's one unpaid stripe protection against when it comes to giving orders?

We sit in the car, smoking, getting our nerves back for the drive… we would get on to the Bukit Timah Road and force our way through the refugees and rabble of deserters heading for the docks. We would negotiate the bomb craters and burnt out trucks and with any luck we would not ourselves become a target for the Zero bombers buzzing like flies over dead meat.

We would find Bombardier Spike Milligan at The Raffles Hotel and he would tell us what to do next. But then he was 'bomb happy', wasn't he? So what use was he going to be for us?

Our Aussie attachment, Bill Partridge, looks out at the pall of smoke rising over the city from a multitude of fires, many started by ourselves to deny the Japs stores when they took over, though we were under orders to resist at all costs.

'If you ask me, Diggers, we should be making tracks out of this neck of the woods. We should be thinking Durban, and Durban nurses…'

'Nobody asked you, Bill, so belt up.'

'Right you are. But you won't get a better idea all day.'

We push the Hudson saloon back on to the road. Dickens gets the engine started and we all climb in. Milligan was mad, we all knew that, but he was Our War – our man in contact with the chain of command that reached right back to Whitehall, even to Winston Churchill.

Winston Churchill was taking a bath, smoking a cigar and drinking from a balloon glass of brandy. He blew out a cloud of Havana smoke and reflectively watched it mingle with the steam above.

'We're fucked,' he said. 'Cancel that last consignment of toilet rolls to Singapore.'

Milligan had other ideas. He was in the cocktail bar of Raffles Hotel having a drink with his CO.

'If we lose here, sir, it's not so bad. We'll arrange a rematch on the Isle of Wight. We're bound to win next time with the crowd behind us.'

EPILOGUE

Spike said, 'Tell the Pope. A full life can be lived by a baby who stays a minute on earth, and an empty life by a fool stretching out his years. I've always sided with innocence, not the innocence of those judged not guilty, but the innocence of those who have not yet been taught to feel guilty.

'I'm with the kids. The jelly wobblers!

'And tell Shelagh my wallet's in the deep freeze under the frozen peas...'

Spike: Early one morning. Running on the track at Alexandra Palace, I felt marvellous. It was a moment when I felt wonderful. There was no-one else out there. The best moment in my life. Just running on that track in the early morning...

There was Spike

There was me

There was me and Spike

Then there was me…